WILL AMERICA SOBER UP?

WILL AMERICA
SOBER UP?

Allan Luks

Beacon Press Boston

Excerpts from this book have appeared in *America, Commonweal, The Futurist, The Report* of the Hastings Center on Ethics, and *Social Policy.*

Copyright ©1983 by Allan Luks

Beacon Press books are published under the auspices
of the Unitarian Universalist Association of Congregations
in North America, 25 Beacon Street, Boston, Massachusetts 02108

Published simultaneously in Canada by
Fitzhenry & Whiteside Limited, Toronto

Printed in the United States of America

(hardcover) 9 8 7 6 5 4 3 2 1

Library of Congress Cataloging in Publication Data

Luks, Allan.
    Will America sober up?
    Bibliography: p.
    Includes index.
    1. Alcoholism — United States. I. Title.
RC565.L84 1983 362.2'92'0973 82-73964
ISBN 0-8070-2154-7

Contents

INTRODUCTION

*Why answers now exist for the world's largest,
costliest and oldest drug problem.*

1

Chapter 1

ALCOHOL AND HEALTH: A MOVEMENT FORMS

*A national education campaign that can help an
individual and a nation to drink moderately.*

7

Chapter 2

THE DEALCOHOLIZED BEVERAGE TEST

*Testing the new dealcoholized drinks indicates
Americans are ready to accept a new style of
consumption.*

20

Chapter 3

NEW PUBLIC POLICIES

*Higher alcohol taxes and other federal actions
can sharply reduce the tragedies of drunkenness
— but is the public willing to let Washington intervene to change the way it drinks?*

42

Chapter 4

A CURE FOR DRUNKENNESS?

Will drinkers even be willing to take a sober-up pill?

62

Chapter 5

COMPULSORY TREATMENT: NEW HELP FOR THE ALCOHOLIC

Laws can get alcoholics into early treatment without waiting for them to "hit bottom."

68

Chapter 6

AN ALCOHOLISM TEST?

Research promises to identify alcoholic children before they ever drink.

109

Chapter 7

THE ETHICS OF IT ALL

The protections that have to be built into these new campaigns, policies, laws and scientific techniques which will affect the lives of every American.

114

Chapter 8

WHAT NOW?

*How to choose healthy, moderate drinking for
yourself — which can influence government to make moderate drinking a national
behavior.*

142

APPENDIX A.   EXCERPTS FROM COERCIVE
TREATMENT REGULATIONS AND
AN INTERNATIONAL OPINION SURVEY

173

APPENDIX B.   THE GALLUP POLL RESULTS

*The data from the Gallup survey that shows a
health-aware nation is more concerned
about drinking than smoking, diet or exercise.
Supports higher taxes on alcohol beverages.
Wants ingredients labels. And will vote for
politicians involved in these issues.*

181

BIBLIOGRAPHY

193

INDEX

203

ACKNOWLEDGMENTS

213

WILL AMERICA SOBER UP?

Introduction

It is September 1982, and every morning this week a national TV show, "Good Morning America," has highlighted the tragedies of drunk driving, and last week *Newsweek*'s cover story of September 13 also focused on this major cause of death among the nation's young. Secretary of Health and Human Services Richard Schweiker recently announced plans to launch a national awareness campaign about teenage problem drinking. The U.S. Senate just approved a resolution designating a "National Drunk and Drugged Driving Awareness Week" every December (which President Reagan would sign).

These are just a few of the month's more publicized activities aimed at checking alcohol's tragedies. As the 1980s begin the headlines show that the nation now realizes that alcohol abuse is by far its greatest drug problem.

"As far as I can determine, there has never in the history of this country . . . been the attention to and concern about alcohol, its use, its marketing, its social impact, its costs in human life and suffering," William Mayer, administrator of the Alcohol, Drug Abuse and Mental Health Administration, said recently.

America has 100 million drinkers and only a fraction of this number need to drink too much and experience accidents for the publicized disasters to continue. Each year alcohol abuse for excessive drinking is involved in 69 percent of the nation's drownings and 83 percent of accidental fire fatalities, and it causes 10 million job accidents and 25,000 traffic deaths. In 1981, the Surgeon General announced that America's death rate dropped 20 percent from 1960 to 1978, except for young people ages 15 to 24 where it grew by 11 percent. The major reason: drunken accidents.

Ethanol is a drug, and more people are affected by its abuse than by all other drug misuse. Consequences of alcohol problems — treatment, accidents, welfare, lost productivity, crime — now cost an economically strapped nation $49.4 billion a year compared to $16.4 billion for all other drug problems, according to the latest study by the National Institute on Alcohol Abuse and Alcoholism.

The public is now very aware of the 10 million drinkers who are addicted to alcohol. Alcoholics are *continual* alcohol abusers. They become psychologically addicted and are nervous, angry, anxious when not drinking. Often they become physically addicted, shaking, sweating, even hallucinating when their bodies have been cut off from ethanol.

Like all drug addicts, only a minority — 15 percent — of alcoholics willingly enter treatment each year. Yet without help, alcoholics eventually destroy their lives as well as the lives of people around them. Alcoholism is responsible for a staggering 12 percent of the nation's costs for adult health services.

In recent years the public learned how the nation's most powerful leaders were touched by alcoholism: former President Jimmy Carter's brother and former President Gerald Ford's wife; the wives of Senators Ted Kennedy and Howard Baker; President Reagan's father. One of the most powerful congressmen, Wilbur Mills, had to resign his position as chairman of the House Ways and Means Committee in 1976 because of his intoxicated behavior, including being stopped for drunk driving with strip-tease dancer Fanne Fox. Press reports were amused but also horrified at Mills' inability to control his drinking. Mills, who went for treatment and is now a recovered alcoholic, told this writer he believes Congress might have approved a national health insurance bill in 1974, except by then his drinking prevented him from effectively guiding this legislation.

Will America Sober Up? shows that the nation *now* has the ability to support a variety of policies, laws, and scientific research that can dramatically reduce the occurrence of alcohol abuse and alcoholism.

Yet considering the toll alcohol problems have long inflicted, an author is especially wary when discussing breakthrough solutions. Alcohol abuse represents the world's oldest drug problem, dating back in Biblical times to a drunk Noah, who when sick and angry from too much wine, fought with his youngest son Ham, and later cursed and condemned Ham's son Canaan to slavery.

Another uneasiness that affects someone discussing solutions to alcohol's tragedies comes from the possibility of being mistaken as a member of the Moral Majority or other organization which preaches that only by adopting values which agree with the group's standards can America wipe away its social ills. This book, however, does not discuss the need for people to change their personal beliefs, but rather for government and citizens to join together to educate alcohol consumers about how they can enjoy healthier lives, to help limit a powerful industry's negative social impact, and to make sure ill people get treatment.

The recommendations may sound controversial: inviting government to tax stiffly alcohol beverages, developing a sober-up pill that would be served at parties, pressuring legally competent alcoholics to get therapy, launching a national campaign against drunkenness while encouraging people to drink with meals, identifying alcoholic children before they ever taste alcohol, creating a new political force focused on alcohol abuse's solutions.

But these proposals have grown out of the experiences of health professionals and recovered alcoholics, people who understand, work with, and are dedicated to helping individuals with alcohol problems. The book also discusses the safeguards that can be placed on these new measures in order to judge them continually by one test: the rights of the individual.

Why have the answers to alcohol's problems appeared only now? The reason is simply that the public sensitivity, scientific knowledge and shared experiences that underlie these solutions did not exist until recently.

One major new force, for example, has been the health awareness that has swept the nation, causing people to change eating and drinking patterns in order to live longer and look and feel better. And, as the book reveals, Americans have now begun to question their alcohol habits and look for ways to moderate drinking.

Also, it was not until the 1960s that medical groups began increasingly to define alcoholism as a progressive illness and complicated drug addiction requiring therapy. This challenged the view held by many that the alcoholic was just a weak person who could stop drinking if only he or she wanted to. Unlike its attitude toward personality disorders, society expects illnesses to be cured, and believes government policies should foster the search for these solutions to better health.

Since alcoholism was now recognized as an illness, companies stopped firing alcoholic employees and insisted they take sick time and get treatment. If the alcoholic refused, he or she was terminated. These intervention efforts in corporations and unions expanded dramatically in the 1970s. The success in getting alcoholics into treatment and sober has now made legislators realize that laws can pressure great numbers of legally competent alcoholics to seek help.

At conferences ten years ago, alcoholism experts would explain the unknowns about the illness. Why, for example, does one drinker become addicted to alcohol and another person drink without losing control? (Alcoholism's causation remains unidentified, but is believed to have physical, emotional, and cultural sources.)

In the last few years, medical research has developed an explanation: Drunkenness is linked to the membrane or lining that covers brain cells, and its distortion by alcohol in turn alters the flow of the brain's impulses. These studies suggest that the alcoholic's cell membrane is affected differently than the non-alcoholic's. This has prompted leading researchers to predict that there will be a way to physically identify alcoholics before they ever drink, then give them counseling and perhaps certain injections to prevent their becoming alcoholic.

Finally, the fiasco of Prohibition is now a half-century old. It has lost its ability to make health professionals too uncomfortable to consider government regulations that would curb alcohol abuse. A recent federally-funded study by a National Research Council panel supporting such initiatives is titled *Alcohol and Public Policy: Beyond the Shadow of Prohibition.*

These research findings and proposals that promise to slice into the nation's alcohol problems have so far surfaced primarily in publications and conferences for professionals. The public is largely unaware that it now can choose many new ways to move against alcoholism as well as to moderate its own drinking.

I have personally seen the new measures work. I have watched heavy as well as average drinkers, caught up by the nation's new health concern, significantly reduce their consumption — and calories — after receiving education about drinking for taste rather than to get high. I have seen the surprise as drinkers realized they had been enjoying, and even getting "high" on, the new dealcoholized beverages.

Angry alcoholics, from welfare recipients to successful businessmen, have come to the health agency that I direct because of a legal threat to suspend their assistance payments or driver's license unless they take treatment. Several have physically threatened my staff. Yet some of these mandated patients have visited me after they completed therapy, to thank me for my agency's help in saving their lives.

Leprosy, typhoid, tuberculosis, and polio are illnesses that once appeared uncontrollable. Societies helplessly watched their ravages. A time came when solutions appeared, involving the adoption of new personal habits, medical treatments, and public policies.

Now the time has arrived when alcohol abuse and alcoholism,

which scar millions of individuals as well as the entire nation, can be dramatically reduced. But are Americans ready to accept the often controversial steps needed to curb alcohol's tragedies?

1

Alcohol and Health: A Movement Forms

In the same way that it covers other national ills, the media focuses on a hot alcohol issue by pouring time and space on it for a limited period — and then racing off after the next new-girl-in-town drinking topic.

About six years ago the hot subject was women and alcohol. As women increasingly work and mix equally with men, will the stigma that society has placed on women who drink excessively disappear, resulting in more female alcohol problems?

I was frequently asked this question by reporters who came to the alcohol abuse prevention agency that I direct. In response I explained that those religious and cultural groups in America that had few alcohol problems limited most of their drinking to social and ritual celebrations. Since accepted restrictions can influence drinking behavior, socially liberated women might experience more alcohol-caused problems.

But then I quickly asked: Why must working women join a society that drinks too much? Why can't America moderate the way it drinks, instead of producing a steady flow of headlines about alcohol-caused tragedies?

The journalists, however, slapped shut their notebooks and TV interviewers nodded to the cameramen to flip off their switches. My last questions were not newsworthy. "Wishful thinking about the big picture is what you helping-types are supposed to do," one TV reporter joked.

About three years ago, the media's interest in drinking problems jumped from women to teenagers. What projects could stop excessive drinking by adolescents?

I told reporters about the need to make young people aware that alcohol is a drug which distorts the brain's ability to think and react; that a bottle of beer — youth's preferred drink — has just as much alcohol as a shot of liquor or a glass of wine; that teenagers tend to gulp their drinks when together, straining the body, which can break down alcohol only at the rate of about one drink an hour, and resulting in extra alcohol rushing through the blood and hitting the brain, often making young drinkers appear foolish and act dangerously. Drunk accidents have become the greatest killer of the nation's youth.

The major influence that shapes teenage drinking habits, however, is the way parents drink (friends are the second influence), I added. The real answer to youthful alcohol abuse is not information, efforts in school and the media, but for adults to drink moderately, enough to enjoy the taste and relaxing effects of an alcoholic beverage, but not until intoxicating euphoria is reached.

My interviewers again dismissed this goal of a moderately drinking nation as pie in the sky. They challenged me by saying, "Does that mean you believe the trend to raise state drinking ages from eighteen to nineteen, twenty or twenty-one isn't needed?"

Higher drinking ages reduce teenage drunk driving accidents, I responded, and so should be supported. However, these laws attack a symptom — drunk driving — and not the model for teenage alcohol problems. And that is American drinking habits. Too many people consume alcohol in order to feel intoxicated, seeing it as a quick self-medication for stress and a necessity for celebrating and being happy, rather than as a complement to entertainment and meals. Israel, for example, reports an alcoholism rate of .2 percent of its population, while America has a 5 percent rate — 25 times higher. Yet Israel has no legal drinking age.

"Jews and Italians are noted for having low drinking

problems," my interviewers replied. "You can't expect that their moderate drinking habits will ever be adopted here."

But I do! I responded, and so do many other health professionals. The hard-news seeking reporters gazed out my office window.

As I now write, the media's hot alcohol topic is drunk driving. Enraged parents whose children have been killed in drunk driving accidents have organized themselves and focused government's attention on the need to stop this continuous carnage. President Reagan has established a Commission on Drunk Driving, which has called for all states to adopt a twenty-one-year-old drinking age as well as stiff penalties and long license suspensions for drunk drivers.

While tough laws are needed, we need to go beyond relieving the symptom, I again have been telling reporters. The cause of alcohol abuse feeds on itself; children follow the pattern set by their parents. But there could and should be a national campaign to eliminate such alcohol abuse.

Although newspaper stories still often fail to mention these comments about changing the nation's drinking habits, journalists now usually ask me to explain how this moderate drinking goal could be achieved. Notes for a possible big picture report are at least being filed. Ralph Lowenstein, host of a morning TV show, "New York, New York," recently said to me after an interview: "The difference that I see now is that people are starting to feel comfortable enough to tell friends to stop drinking so much. They want change."

John Volpe, former Secretary of Transportation and chairman of the President's Commission on Drunk Driving, said despite that group's call for stricter enforcement, the real answer "must go far beyond the highway environment to the heart of the problem — society's values, attitudes and behaviors regarding the use and abuse of alcohol."

In 1982, my alcohol abuse prevention agency commissioned a Gallup poll that asked Americans whether they wanted national campaigns to eliminate smoking, teach proper diet and exercise behaviors, and create moderate drinking habits.

A national health effort to stop excessive drinking was the one supported by the most people; 68 percent of those surveyed felt such a campaign was "very important" and 90 percent rated it as at least "somewhat important" (see Appendix B).

A Movement Starts

"In the next decade one can predict that increasing attention will be paid to this model [government-directed efforts to moderate consumption] and that it will become a major cornerstone of the alcohol policy in many countries, especially in Scandinavia . . . in Canada and perhaps the United States," says Dr. David Pittman, sociology research director at Washington University in St. Louis and a veteran researcher on the problems of alcohol abuse.

"A swing back of public opinion, away from complete liberalization and towards a reasonable degree of alcohol control, has been noted in recent years," concludes a survey of eighty nations done by the World Health Organization and Canada's Addiction Research Foundation, the leading private institution concerned with preventing alcohol problems.

The nation's powerful liquor industry, which provided $6.7 billion in taxes in 1980 to local, state, and federal governments and usually can make politicians listen to its concerns, is worried. The 1982 annual meeting of the industry's trade association called this drive for moderation a new "anti-alcohol movement."

The health professionals who advocate government education as well as regulations limiting how much people drink belong to a trend rather than any organized movement. Supporters visualize this sentiment growing into not only an identifiable movement but also a political force, whose banner would demand a more moderate life style, and confronting big business and government on many related social ills (see chapter 8). The liquor industry's trade group, the Distilled Spirits Council of the United States, claims that this move to limit consumption will lead to "the radical restructuring of the regulatory environment."

The alcohol beverage industry labels as "Neo-Prohibition-ist" anyone, in government or private health care, who favors attempts to change the nation's drinking practices. The beer, wine, and liquor companies quickly paint an advocate as a throwback to the failed Prohibition movement, as an illiberal, morality preacher who wants massive government regulation of private behavior.

When Milton Terris, past president of the American Public Health Association, announced to that group in 1966 that he supported "governmental, fiscal, and regulatory measures to reduce per capita alcohol consumption," he was met with discomfort and jokes. Others present called out about "having a drink or two" before Terris's views became law.

Remembering this reaction, Dan Beauchamp, associate professor of health administration at the University of North Carolina, explains that in the intervening years this sentiment has given way along with the withering of Prohibition's memory: health professionals now feel comfortable enough to speak out for government advocacy of consumption limits that lessen the tragedy of alcohol abuse without eliminating drinking.

The Neo-Prohibitionist tag in fact appears to anger rather than dissuade. Mark Worden, associate editor of the magazine *Alcoholism,* recently wrote: "Obviously the (Neo)prohibi-tionist displays none of the hardy outdoor athletic vigor of the beer drinker. None of the sensitivity of the bon vivant oeno-phile. None of the strong allure and charm of those who quaff spirits.

"If you speak favorably about the common good sense of contents labeling and health hazard warnings for alcoholic beverages you are a troglodyte. Same thing if you talk about stabilizing or reducing per capita consumption."

The new drive to eliminate excessive drinking represents a humanist approach to the problem of alcohol abuse. Its supporters reject this Neo-Prohibitionist label, since they believe society can enjoy alcohol without its problems.

In contrast, Prohibition's sentiment was rigid, intolerant, and fatalistic. No one could control his or her drinking once started. All drinking had to be eliminated. Prohibition's supporters angrily rejected any violator, from a husband to the president of the United States. A letter to the editor in the December 5, 1924, issue of the *Valley Express,* the newspaper of Valley Junction, Iowa, by Mrs. Nell Geiselhart, declared:

Had I been so unfortunate as to have married a drunkard there would have been just one time and one time only for that sot to have come home liquored up.

Some fathers think, who have become dissipated, that their sons do not know about it. Your son knows all about it. I have heard profane men say: I am profane, but never in the presence of my children. Your children know you are profane. Time will pass on. Your son will be sixteen or seventeen years of age. He will shove back from the evening meal, light a cigar and go out somewhere to spend his evenings. You will hear nothing of him until you hear him coming in after midnight. His constitution may not be so strong as yours and the liquor he drinks so terrifically drugged so that he will catch up with you on the road to death, and you both can go to Hades together, although you may have had a long start on him.

Within President Harding's and President Wilson's administrations an article was published in one of our daily papers that one of our anti-saloon or temperance lecturers had said that when President Wilson moved out of the White House he had to have a permit to move his wines out, and that when President Harding moved in he had to have a permit to move his wines in, and this lecturer defied either man to deny it. There has been much scandal concerning the booze movement at Washington, D.C., and there seems to be something rotten in Denmark, and as all our eyes are turned on our national capital, the fountainhead of our present government, will history reveal in years to come that some of our great men were wine bibblers.

That same four-page edition of the *Valley Express* contained an obituary that revealed the Midwest's strong, religious-tinged fatalism, which gave Prohibition its roots:

The funeral of George Cline of Seventh and Walnut streets, who died Saturday evening at his home, was held on

Tuesday morning at 10 o'clock, Rev. Brooks officiating at the church and burial was at Indianola. Mr. Cline had been in poor health for several years, but was not in a dangerous condition until about three weeks ago, when he came home from church and fell on the floor as he stepped in the door.

Today's advocates of a national effort backed by Washington to moderate consumption explain they are not preaching anti-drinking or morality. The goal is moderation not elimination.

Supporters admit that their attack on America's drinking habits would not eliminate alcoholism, an illness of unknown cause that leaves 10 million people addicted, unable to control their drinking, and needing therapy that leads to abstinence. Rather, a national moderate-drinking campaign would be aimed at America's 90 million other drinkers who are physically able to control their consumption, but who when drinking excessively risk becoming a federal statistic. Excessive drinking is involved in 70 percent of deaths from falls, 69 percent of drownings, 83 percent of fatal fire accidents, 40 percent of accidental deaths on the job, 50 percent of highway fatalities, 52 percent of spouse beatings, and 38 percent of child abuse.

According to local as well as federal studies, alcohol-related problems are increasing. In Minnesota this toll grows about 6 percent each year, concluded an in-depth study of Minnesota's statistics in such areas as deaths, arrests, and hospital admissions. Dr. Joseph Westermeyer, a medical doctor, and the other authors from the University of Minnesota state, "It stretches the imagination to believe that thousands of reporting sources throughout the state, representing different disciplines, and reporting in different modes to different agencies, should, in concert, erroneously report (these) rates."

Moderate drinking is defined as averaging not more than two drinks a day by the National Institute on Alcohol Abuse and Alcoholism (NIAAA). Fifteen million adults — 15 percent of the nation's drinkers — average more than two drinks of beer, wine, or liquor each day, usually far more. They consume half of all the alcohol sold in America. Fifteen percent of all men and 3 percent of all women who drink average at least four drinks daily and are "drinking at substantial risk for the development of either alcoholism or serious problem drinking," the NIAAA states.

Alcohol's effects vary with body weight (a heavier person requires slightly more alcohol before becoming drunk), emotional make-up, and the drinking environment, but anyone can drink too much at some time and go on to become an alcohol abuse statistic. "The probability of experiencing a serious incident rises from 6.5 percent at the lowest consumption level (an average of less than a half a drink daily) to 52.2 percent at the highest consumption level (more than ten drinks a day)," according to the NIAAA's 1981 report *Alcohol and Health*.

The New Education

A national campaign to moderate the nation's drinking will succeed, explain supporters, because it is based on and will offer new knowledge rather than moral preaching. Studies have questioned, for example, why those Americans with traditionally few alcohol problems — Jews, Italians and Orientals — are now experiencing an increase in alcohol abuse. The research concludes that these populations always placed a strong taboo on drunkenness while at the same time demonstrating to their children that alcohol was a natural part of meals and celebrations (rather than self-medication necessary to relax and relieve stress). This teaching is disappearing because of acculturation, the general decline of parental influence, and the retreat from religious practice and rituals.

Why can't government, along with private health agencies, step in and try to educate an entire nation in the same way these groups once taught their young? ask the new moderation proposals. Campaigns in the media and schools would teach appropriate drinking habits, while attaching strong negative values to anyone who drank too much and became intoxicated.

Present paid and public-service announcements on TV and in magazines, however, offer a nonjudgmental theme with wide latitude for drinkers: "eat before you drink," "know your limits," and "drink responsibly." Prohibition's legacy and the alcohol beverage industry's strong influence on the media has restrained public messages from offering specific rules to limit drinking or judgments on drunkenness.

A recent full-page advertisement in *Reader's Digest* by Operation Cork, which is the wealthiest foundation involved in alcohol abuse and funded by the millions of the Kroc family of McDonald hamburgers, shows a little girl saying, "I worry when Mommy and Daddy drive after they've had too much to drink." But exactly what is too much? Such indefinite themes, complain the moderate-drinking supporters, neither make the reader-drinker experience shame or guilt — as Jews and Italians have made their children feel — when consuming excessively nor educate him or her about the when, where, and how much of safe drinking.

The new proposals instead want intensive public awareness campaigns, aimed especially at the young, emphasizing that drunkenness is not just to be avoided but also is distasteful, a sign of a lack of self-control, and an embarrassment to the drinker, his or her family, and friends. A British effort aimed at heavy-drinking families in northern England emphasizes: "The northeast drinks more than any other area in the country and it's got more problems because of it!"

Announcements in the media and distributed in schools would recommend specific drinking patterns: enjoy alcohol at social functions and when with others; drink with meals, but do not drink quickly, when alone, in reaction to problems, or before driving. The messages would propose drinking limits, based on the body's ability to break down alcohol at the rate of a drink an hour. A French campaign has told citizens not to have more than two glasses of wine with their main meal.

Such a national education campaign would confront the long-standing themes of the beer, wine, and liquor industries, which emphasize that drinking makes individuals attractive and more drinking makes people more attractive. Beverages are advertised for "When you're having more than one." The World Health Organization has endorsed this confrontation, describing it as "value education rather than information, and the values and norms tend to stress moderation, the avoidance of excess, and the personal responsibility for one's behavior."

A new awareness effort also would include general information. A report by the U.S. Department of the Treasury on health hazards associated with alcohol notes: "Numerous information gaps and substantial misinformation relating to alcohol use exist among the American public. People are unaware of the effects rapid consumption can have on the body . . ."

Combining alcohol information with announcements offering healthy drinking practices as well as value-laden attacks on drunkenness is meant to build into the population a learned instinct that triggers guilt when someone feels himself becoming drunk or recognizes he is starting to drink in an inappropriate way.

In a study of such sects as the National Unification Church ("the Moonies"), which frown on drinking although they do not formally preach abstinence, Dr. Marc Galanter, of Mt. Sinai Hospital in New York, found that youths joining these groups felt relief at having a clear behavior standard for alcohol and decreased their drinking sharply. "An individual's alcohol-related attitudes will come to conform to the norms of the large group," he concluded.

To what extent will a *nation* change its excessive drinking habits in response to an intensive education campaign that actually encourages moderate consumption values and techniques?

The Education Campaign's Arguments

Media stories about alcohol abuse's tragedies, such as those surrounding the drunkenness-caused deaths in 1981 of film stars William Holden (from a fall) and Natalie Wood (a drowning), appear to have little impact on alcohol use. The headlines just repeat themselves, writes Elisabeth Kübler-Ross in *On Death and Dying*: "Since we cannot perceive our own immortality, news of people killed in battles, in wars, on the highways, only supports our unconscious belief in our own immortality."

Fighting this "unconscious belief" by creating a learned instinct against excessive drinking makes sense only in theory, declare opponents of the reduced consumption proposals, such as Professor Pittman of Washington University, whose research has been funded by the liquor industry as well as the federal government. "We haven't come out publicly on these control of consumption reports," says Paul Gavaghan, an executive with the liquor industry's trade association. "But Pittman's work is the one that coincides with our views."

Pittman argues, "Jewish cultural emphasis on sobriety while encouraging moderate consumption of alcohol does suggest that indoctrination of values is significant, but research has not demonstrated whether such values are generalized or specific in nature." His doubt that moderate consumption values can ever be accepted generally in a multicultural country like the United States comes from international comparisons: Spain, Italy, and Portugal, for example, report a higher per capita consumption of alcohol than Norway, Finland, and Sweden. Yet the Scandinavian nations have a greater incidence of alcohol abuse problems, primarily because of culturally ingrained drinking habits.

Supporters of efforts to stop excessive drinking believe, however, that cultural blending in the United States has become widespread enough to allow the acceptance of national norms about good health. For proof they point to the new health fitness attitudes which have been adopted by members of all population groups as well as the cultural shading which has overridden the centuries-old traditional restrictions against excessive drinking held by the Jews, Italians, and others.

Many opponents, at least those outside the alcohol beverage industry, will admit that Scandinavian nations, Scandinavians in America, and other U.S. cultures with high rates of alcohol problems might change their drinking practices in response to a prolonged national awareness effort aimed at creating a taboo on drunkenness and providing definite norms on how and when to use alcohol. Still they argue that, on balance, such a large and unproven campaign should not be attempted since in addition to possibly failing, it could bring back Prohibition's intolerance.

Groups that accept the new drinking habits may attack those who refuse. The Protestants' reformist zeal during Prohibition often broke out in religious bigotry against the Catholic and Jewish immigrants in the cities. Frustrated bureaucrats could harass non-moderate drinking populations.

Reviewing the history of Prohibition in Michigan, Larry Englemann, in his study *Intemperance,* writes about a group of wealthy Michigan residents: "Harassed, assaulted, and insulted, they discovered that their lives and property were suddenly endangered not so much by lawbreakers as by the crude, rough-talking, rowdy, and rude individuals selected to enforce the law."

Englemann quotes from a poem "The Patriot's Prayer," written by Arthur Lippman:

> Now I lay me down to sleep —
> My life and limb may Hoover keep,
> And may no Coast Guard cutter shell
> This little home I love so well.
> May no dry agent, shooting wild,
> Molest mine wife and infant child,
> Or searching out some secret still,
> Bombard my home to maim and kill.
> When dawn succeeds the gleaming stars,
> May we devoid of wounds and scars,
> Give thanks we didn't fall before
> The shots in Prohibition's War.

Supporters of efforts to limit consumption reply that their proposals have no connection to Prohibition's attempt to institute both laws and a morality that would eliminate all drinking. Actually encouraging drinking at such times as meals and celebrations, their program will lead to an atmosphere of moderation.

Proponents admit that their campaign would have to be long lasting before its success or failure could be determined. Jewish values on moderation go far back. Maimonides, the twelfth century Spanish rabbi, physician, and philosopher, wrote when trying to codify ancient oral law: "Lest a person says: Since jealousy, lust and desire for honor are evil ways . . . I will separate myself completely from them and go to the other extreme, to the point where he refuses to enjoy the pleasure of food by abstaining from eating meat and drinking wine, where he refuses to marry a wife, or to live in a pleasant house or to wear nice clothing but instead chooses to dress in rags . . . *this too is an evil way, and it is forbidden to go that way.*"

"In the Jewish scriptures, wine is also a gift from God, even a blessing, but it must be used at the proper time and only in moderation," conclude two Queens College sociologists, John O'Brien and Sheldon Seller, in a study of the Old Testament. "The only drunks (in the Old Testament)," says Seller, "are Lot and Noah, who lived before the covenant and therefore were not really Jewish."

A long-lasting effort to place a taboo on drunkenness could increase the stigma alcoholics feel, argue the foes of a national moderate drinking program. Believing society sees them as morally weak for not controlling their drinking, alcoholics deny they have an addiction, with only 15 percent of the nation's 10 million alcoholics seeking treatment each year for their often fatal illness.

The counterargument is that if society truly accepts a strong onus against becoming intoxicated, it will affect all drinkers not just the alcoholic. Among the nation's 100 million drinkers, obviously any drinker can get drunk. An anti-drunkenness campaign would result in alcoholics recognizing that many other people experience problems with alcohol and so lessen their resistance to help.

2

The Dealcoholized Beverage Test

"You want to be another Billy Sunday?" That jest greeted Paul Screvane, a well-known New York Democratic leader, when he visited some legislators not long ago to talk about alcohol abuse.

A political pro who was City Council president and once ran for mayor, Screvane enjoyed drinking and was definitely no teetotaler. When an acquaintance became an alcoholic, Screvane saw the resulting misery firsthand and added excessive alcohol use to his many social concerns. Still, drinking problems were not his first priority and he spent relatively little time on them.

"Yet my political friends kidded me, calling me Billy Sunday, when we met privately," Screvane remembers. "It shows the uphill fight we have to change the attitudes of politicians."

The elected official's reluctance to become involved with drinking questions other than those in which the public has already expressed an interest — for example, the legal drinking age and tougher drunk driving laws — comes from fear of being ridiculed. Officials know well that the public often sees them as stereotypes, especially on critical issues. Their uneasiness would obviously be heightened if asked to promote a national awareness campaign to moderate drinking. Supporters have been ridiculed already as Neo-Prohibitionists by the powerful alcohol beverage industry.

Since it is always difficult to know when public opinion is truly changing, politicians view society cautiously through presently accepted attitudes. Yet officials like to champion changes early, in order to earn the recognition that the public and media give innovative leaders. And supporters of moderate consumption argue that the country is ready to embrace their policies.

But where can politically sensitive leaders find proof that a society that cheered Prohibition's repeal just fifty years ago is ready to accept a national campaign aimed at dramatically changing its alcohol practices? Perhaps the moderate-consumption supporters are the ones completely out of touch. The famous warning of Erasmus to public officials hangs in many government offices: "It is a good part of sagacity to have known the foolish desires of the crowd and their unreasonable notions."

Yet there is visible evidence that U.S. attitudes have changed markedly. Consider, for example, the traditional American dinner of meat and potatoes. Now fish and salads are replacing this basic piece of American identity. What about the importance of coffee to Americans — the early-morning pick-me-up or the coffee break at work which has provoked strikes when limits have been placed on it? Increasingly varieties of decaffeinated coffee as well as decaffeinated tea crowd supermarket shelves and are offered in the best restaurants. The world's leader in lacing its foods and drinks with sugar and salt, the United States has become the leading producer of substitutes for sugar and salt. Purchasers regularly reject foods and beverages with artificial ingredients that they, their parents, and even grandparents once bought routinely and instead substitute all-natural brands.

Credit these changes to the nation's dramatic new health awareness. The desire to feel better, look younger, and live longer has become a powerful influence on what Americans put into their bodies. This strong force now appears ready to change another well-entrenched U.S. habit that affects millions — consuming too much alcohol.

The New Health and Alcohol Moderation

The 1982 Gallup survey found that 68 percent of Americans believed it was "very important" for the nation to teach moderate/sensible drinking habits, and that this sentiment was greater than efforts to curb smoking or encourage proper diet/exercise. Public behavior, though, does not always follow opinion polls' predictions. The reaction to the health substitute for alcohol, which carries the label "dealcoholized," is visible evidence of America's new attitude toward drinking. Gourmet food shops have for some time stocked champagnelike bottles of carbonated grape juice and cans containing a mixture of water, malt, corn, yeast, and hops. Except for the packaging, these alcohol-free imitations did not resemble wine and beer, especially in the crucial area of taste.

New dealcoholized beverages, however, are first fully fermented and brewed and then their alcohol is separated out — usually by rapidly decreased pressure — to less than an unnoticeable 0.5 percent, the federal maximum before classifying a drink as alcoholic. The full taste and body remain.

With a beverage that has less than a half a percent of alcohol, a drinker would need to consume twenty-four glasses of dealcoholized wine or eight cans of beer to obtain the same amount of alcohol as in one four-ounce glass of wine (12 percent alcohol) or one twelve-ounce can of beer (4 percent alcohol). Intoxication becomes impossible. (The alcohol content in a regular can of beer goes from about 4 to 5 percent; a glass of wine ranges from about 8 to 12 percent.)

The drinker also reduces his or her calories per drink by around 60 percent. A regular glass of beer has about 150 calories, and wine carries 80 (dry wines) to 150 calories (dessert wines). Dealcoholized beer contains 40-65 and wine 30-40 calories respectively. The prices of the alcoholic and dealcoholized beverages are the same.

If American drinking society embraces these new beverages, it would show, in addition to the opinion polls, that the public would not throw "Billy Sunday" and other out-of-date labels at politicians who advance policies to alter drinking patterns in the name of better health. In tests of these new drinks, the public reaction has been very positive.

Introduced in Europe about two years ago, dealcoholized wines are just now entering this country. The *Alcoholic Beverage Newsletter,* a trade publication, has already written: "There is evidence about that the real 'wine revolution' is yet to come in the form of alcohol-free wines."

Dealcoholized beers have been available for a long time for those abstaining for health and religious reasons, but brewers are now marketing them to the drinking public. "When in the last years we saw drinkers go after the new 'light beers' (about 3 percent instead of 4 percent alcohol, and 90 rather than 150 calories), we realized dealcoholized brews can be the next step, and in fact the sale of our alcohol-removed beer is starting to slowly grow," says Bob Leahy, director of marketing for the G. Heileman Brewing Company in Wisconsin. The firm's "light" lesson: less alcohol can satisfy regular drinkers sensitive to better health fitness.

Cathy Zelzer, vice president for marketing of Texas Select, a dealcoholized sixty-five-calorie beer, said recently, "After a series of taste tests and very positive responses, we decided to introduce the product in a few U.S. test markets. To me, Texas Select offers a quality alternative to drinking at a time when an increasing number of people are looking for such alternatives."

On social occasions, with a full bar and everyone wanting to relax, people tend to drink too quickly. Teenagers in a group also feel pressure to keep up with each other's drinking. As a result alcohol is consumed faster than the body can break it down. The alcohol builds up, affects the brain, distorts thinking and perception, and some of the people who have had too many become tragic headlines.

Most drinkers are not alcoholics. Only about 25 percent of arrested drunk drivers are alcoholic, for example. As long as just a small fraction of America's drinking population continues to have a few too many, alcohol abuse will remain one of the nation's major killers.

In the future, a drinker, once he feels socially relaxed from alcohol, could switch to a dealcoholized beverage. He or she would avoid intoxication, yet the enjoyable wine or beer taste could continue and the change in beverage would not be signaled by carrying around a different-looking drink. Teenagers would remain holding golden glasses of nonintoxicating beer.

The analogy is to decaffeinated coffee. Until recently, coffee drinkers disdained this 97 percent caffeine-free substitute. They wanted and needed caffeine's pick-me-up. Until 1958 the National Coffee Association did not even mention decaffeinated coffee in its annual statistics. Now, thanks to the new health consciousness, 14 percent of the population consume 2.4 decaffeinated cups a day — almost a 100 percent increase since 1972. Most buyers, according to the industry, are coffee drinkers who use decaffeinated coffee as a way to cut down on caffeine, while still enjoying the taste of coffee. "In fact, drinkers of decaffeinated coffee are flocking to gourmet and specialty food stores where they pay premium prices — up to $6 a pound — for high quality decaffeinated coffee," writes Chris Lecos, a staff member of the Food and Drug Administration.

The New Drinkers

Will the dealcoholized beverages have the same experience as decaffeinated coffee, attracting regular drinkers rather than just previous abstainers? One positive indication is the light beer experience.

Since 1975, when light beer first began to be actively promoted, sales of the low-calorie, low-alcohol beers have jumped 80 percent compared to a 19 percent growth in overall beer purchases. "As it stands, the 12 to 15 percent share of the beer market that the light beers enjoy has come at the expense of the regular beers," says Marvin Shanken, publisher of several trade publications.

Light or low-calorie beer drinkers described their drinking values in a study by Thomas Manning, a consultant to the beer industry, "in terms of *weight concern* ('for people worried about their weight'), *consumption level* ('good to have when drinking a lot of beer') and as an *accompaniment to* food ('good with meals')." Manning concluded that these beverages should become a trend setter: "Compared with other beer drinkers, light beer drinkers are more upscale in income, as well as being younger."

"Similarly, current projections peg low-cal, low-alcohol wines (7 percent alcohol vs. 8-12 percent for regular wine) at a hefty 10 to 15 percent of the market in this decade alone," emphasizes the industry's *Alcoholic Beverage Newsletter.*

A Gallup poll of U.S. drinkers from 1939 to 1979, reported in the Michigan magazine *Bottom Line,* calculated the number of abstainers in 1939, six years after Prohibition's repeal, at 42 percent. The percentage kept dropping until 1978, when it reached 28 percent, but then in 1979, it began to rise slowly, going to 31 percent. The survey's conclusion was that the future could well see Americans drinking less alcohol. The major reason for this is "a growing preoccupation with health and physical fitness."

The dealcoholized beverages satisfy taste as well as the new health concerns. After recently sampling Giovane, an Italian dealcoholized wine fermented from a well-known wine grape, *trebbiano di romagna,* Tedd Thomey, restaurant editor of the Long Beach, California, *Press-Telegram,* wrote, "I never thought a non-alcoholic wine could taste like a real wine. I hope Long Beach restaurants will decide to stock it as an alternate to the harder stuff." The Los Angeles Restaurant and Wine Association selected this wine for its annual banquet.

Perhaps the first tests of whether dealcoholized wines and beers would attract regular drinkers were recently carried out by the New York City Affiliate of the National Council on Alcoholism, a large alcoholism prevention agency, along with other organizations concerned with alcohol abuse. As executive director of the New York organization, I contacted the

Wine Institute in San Francisco, the industry's trade association, which led me to two dealcoholized white wines, Giovane and Castella (from Australia), and the U.S. Brewers Association in Washington, D.C., which identified two dealcoholized beers, Metbrau and Kingsbury (both from America).

I first wanted to check my own impression. Trying both wines at dinner, I did not like the sweet, fruity Australian wine but enjoyed the sparkling Italian one. Both had a distinct advantage over regular wine: without alcohol's distortion of the senses, I enjoyed my food far more.

With the two beers I ate pizza. Drunk very cold, both beers offered the same refreshing, bitter taste of regular beer. All dealcoholized beverages seem to have to be chilled far more than their alcohol counterparts in order to produce an equal taste. The foamy beverages left my stomach with the fullness of beer.

After quickly drinking both cans of beer I felt strange. A waiting pause had entered my body. Then I realized that it was the lack of any effect on my thinking; my mind felt surprisingly clear.

I eventually decided that I preferred dealcoholized wine to regular wine. By avoiding wine's anesthesia, I could taste my food better while also enjoying the flavor of the wine. Regular beer I thought had a better taste, but only slightly. I do not like the feeling of becoming intoxicated, of fighting to keep control over myself, and so I definitely would switch to the dealcoholized beers if I were drinking more than two regular brews.

I especially enjoyed the dealcoholized wine as a late evening drink. My tiring body is not slowed down by alcohol's depressant effects. Rather, I experience a slight pick-me-up feeling, for wine is a far livelier beverage than fruit juice or coffee or tea, and the dealcoholized variety is far more nutritious and less fattening than soda.

I belong to the "light drinker" sector of alcohol purchasers. Studies on U.S. consumption reveal that about one third of all adults abstain. Of the 100 million or two thirds who drink, 50 percent are considered light or infrequent consumers, their weekly intake of distilled spirits, wine, or beer averaging less than a half glass a day. Moderate drinkers — more than 35 percent of all alcohol users — consume between a half to two glasses a day. Heavy imbibers — about 15 percent — take more than two drinks every day, usually far more.

Dealcoholized beer and wine do appeal to those who drink more frequently. One tasting of the Italian wine was done at the Junior League of New York, the well-known organization of women who volunteer their time to charitable causes. Arriving one evening at their headquarters in a beautiful old townhouse off Park Avenue, the women walked up the marble steps to the second floor, many of them ready to enter the wood paneled lounge to buy a drink before attending their meetings. Instead they were greeted by a table set up outside the bar with glasses of the dealcoholized wine.

The women's initial remarks belonged to two types: "Let me hurry and try it so I can go and get the real stuff," and "How fascinating, like decaffeinated coffee. I never realized something like this existed."

Seventy-five women, whose ages ranged from the late twenties to the forties, sipped the wine. According to the survey they then completed, 40 percent were moderate and 20 percent heavy drinkers, while 40 percent classified themselves as light drinkers.

Sixty-nine percent of the women rated the wine good to excellent, although 63 percent said it was not as enjoyable as their regular wine. Asked if they would "consume it as a way to drink less regular wine," 69 percent of the Leaguers said yes. The women saw themselves using a dealcoholized wine most often at business lunches, when socializing for long periods of time, before driving, and at family dinners.

The next testing took place across town, in New York's Hell's Kitchen, that tough section of jammed-together tenements west of the theater district, in a building that serves as a residence for male prisoners on a work-release program. Black and white men, between twenty and forty, the participants in the program, called Chrysalis Place, had committed a wide range of nonviolent crimes.

Half of the twenty-five participants were light drinkers; 25 percent were moderate alcohol consumers; and 25 percent qualified as heavy consumers, saying they took from two to four drinks or more a day. The men's opinions strikingly matched the findings of the Junior League test: Sixty percent of the men liked the wine, but not as much as their regular wine. Seventy percent indicated they would buy it and use it as a way to drink less wine.

The next test involved dealcoholized beer and revealed similar attitudes. Twelve young Harlem fathers, average age twenty-six, who meet monthly to work on community problems, agreed to try the well-chilled, foamy beer. All the men said they enjoyed regular beer, drank it often, and doubted they would like beer with its alcohol removed. Four of the heavy-drinking fathers usually drank between eleven to twenty cans of beer a week, and five fathers said they consumed from four to ten cans a week.

They sipped the dealcoholized beer slowly, surprised and smiling because the taste was almost indistinguishable from regular beer. Three-fourths of the men rated the dealcoholized beer good to excellent; half said it tasted as good as the brew they usually drank; and over half the men said they would buy it.

Only two fathers indicated they would now consider drinking only dealcoholized beer. Yet as in the wine tasting, the majority, seven men, said they definitely would buy and consume the alcohol-free beer from now on as a way to consume less alcohol and calories. They would drink it "at the end of a party," "after a dinner date," "at home with a couple of friends," and "at a party with teenagers."

The next beer tasting took place at a golf club on Long Island Sound. Francis Smithers, a businessman and president of the nonprofit Health Promotion Foundation, which educates the public on health issues, was offered some cold dealcoholized beer and refused it. "I'm sure it's terrible," he said. Finally he agreed to drink it, and sat back in disbelief, saying, "I can't taste the difference."

He agreed to offer it surreptitiously to friends at the exclusive Creek Country Club. Before teeing off, two of his partners, Manhattan executives and regular beer drinkers, ordered beers from the bar. Smithers had arranged for them to receive the dealcoholized beers in cool, frosted glasses. The men were hot, the room was hot, and they enjoyably gulped down the beers, not noticing any difference. When Smithers revealed his secret, the drinkers could not believe they hadn't detected the switch and wanted to know where to buy these beverages.

This three-person golf club experiment is obviously different from the larger wine-tasting or beer-sampling tests. In the other three, the participants knew they were drinking dealcoholized wines and beer, permitting them to imagine differences not really there and so possibly to rate the alcohol-removed beverages too harshly.

Toward the end of the evening at the Junior League, for example, the late arrivals were only told that they could try a new low-calorie wine, and several said after carefully sipping it that they thought it had a "good kick." Dr. Luther Cloud, former associate medical director of the Equitable Life Assurance Society, once offered his staff some beer without telling them it was alcohol-free, and a number told him they felt "high." "Several blind tests verified that most people couldn't tell the difference in taste between Texas Select and their favorite beer," says Cathy Zelzer.

Few people have heard of the dealcoholized beverages. Even many professionals in the alcoholism field are unaware of them, this writer found, when at a recent international conference in Munich he brought a German red alcohol-free wine to the table. "What kind of drink is that?" asked the diners from the United States, Switzerland, France, Sweden, and Britain. Villa Banfi, one of the largest importers of Italian wines, also admitted its ignorance of dealcoholized wines recently. Richard Brown, an assistant to the chairman, John

Mariani, wrote, "but being involved in the exciting growth of pure and natural wines, we learn something every day."

While dealcoholized distilled spirits have not yet appeared — "take alcohol out of liquor and how much taste is left?" a spokesman from the Distilled Spirits Council of the United States asked — dealcoholized wines and beers alone could have a significant impact on excessive alcohol use.

What It Means

Americans consume nearly half of their alcohol, 49 percent, in the form of beer. Wine accounts for 12 percent of the total alcohol consumption and distilled spirits for 39 percent. From 1970 to 1978, beer and wine consumption in the United States grew by about 20 percent, while distilled spirits consumption fell 4 percent. The low-alcohol or "light" wines and beers were their industries' fastest-growing products. The new dealcoholized beverages are riding this taste shift, and their increased use could begin to teach Americans that they can enjoy an alcoholic drink for its flavor rather than euphoria.

The use of dealcoholized beverages also could reduce the number of alcoholics. In nations with low alcoholism rates, such as the Mediterranean countries, people drink primarily to enjoy the beverage's taste rather than to experience the alcohol-induced anesthesia. Such cultural conditioning inhibits heavy drinking in persons physically and/or emotionally predisposed to become alcoholic.

A lower level of national drinking also means that the alcoholic can be more readily identified, by friends, employers, or himself, and made aware of the need for help. When alcoholics get into treatment early, therapy is most successful.

"There is the possibility that Americans will begin to understand wine as a basic food product, rather than as just another spiritous beverage," says California-based wine critic, Richard Paul Hinkle.

The rapid growth of Miller's "Lite" beer is attributed to its campaign, "tastes great, less filling." Normal beer advertising emphasizes heavy drinking: "when you're having more than one." Miller has taught beer drinkers, who originally disdained the diet beers, that they still can be manly while drinking less alcohol.

A survey of 321 New England college students who had experienced alcohol-caused problems because they were "frequent heavy" drinkers — consuming weekly at least five or more cans of beer, four or more glasses of wine, or four or more shots of distilled spirits — found that what most distinguished this group from moderate college drinkers was their motivation, "drinking to get drunk." A study of California colleges found that 35 percent of those students were such heavy drinkers.

That drinking habits now have the potential to be changed dramatically also has been demonstrated abroad. Recent statistics from the state of Bavaria, Germany's beer-drinking center, revealed that between 1976 and 1980 youths aged twelve to twenty-four shifted away from using alcoholic beverages, so that their drinking would not interfere with an active lifestyle. Erich Schuster, a minister of health from Bavaria, reported that the percentage of youngsters regularly consuming fruit juices during these five years rose from 48 to 53 percent; soft drinks, 47 to 52 percent; and mineral water, 24 to 32 percent. The number of youngsters regularly drinking alcoholic beverages, meanwhile, fell significantly: from 17 to 9 percent for twelve to fourteen year olds, 46 to 31 percent for fifteen to seventeen year olds, 56 to 50 percent for eighteen- to twenty-year-olds, and 65 to 54 percent for twenty-one to twenty-four-year-olds.

Reinforcing this trend, the Bavarian government recently passed a law requiring its restaurants, including the famed beer halls and gardens, to offer alcohol-free beverages on the menu and to price some below the cheapest alcoholic drink. Menus previously listed a glass of beer for about $.80 to $1.20, while a soft drink or apple juice, the only alcohol-free choices, ranged in price from $1.50 to $2.50.

The Munich city council even proposed heresy: a requirement that there be pavilions serving alcohol-free beverages among the sea of beer tents at its world-famous Oktoberfest, when more than a million gallons of beer are drunk. The proposal was defeated, however.

The government-owned monopolies that control alcohol sales in Norway and Finland have also pressured their stores as well as restaurants to offer alcohol-free beverages, including dealcoholized wines, on their shelves and menus.

By switching to dealcoholized beverages in restaurants and homes and thus reducing the amount of alcohol consumed, U.S. drinkers could experience what studies have continually affirmed: that a drink or two helps someone relax with other people, but as more alcohol is drunk the drinker becomes less communicative. Also, it has been observed that given nothing stronger than tonic water but told they are drinking alcohol, people will suddenly talk more, exhibit more outgoing and even aggressive behavior, and even become sexually aroused. People can get "high on themselves." It may sound trite, but it is true.

In his new book, *Beyond Alcoholism: Alcohol and Public Health Policy,* Dan Beauchamp, associate professor of health administration at the University of North Carolina, concludes, "The overall goal of alcohol control policy would be to encourage high rates of minimal or non-use of alcohol." The problem is how to gain popular support for government actions to achieve this. Dealcoholized beverages are a way to initiate public involvement in this aim, and their increased use will be a clear sign to officials that the proposals to moderate consumption will not be disdained by society.

Dr. Robert Atkins, the best-selling diet doctor-nutritionist, told a staff member of the New York City Affiliate of the National Council on Alcoholism that dealcoholized beverages "are a million-dollar idea." For drinkers who switch to these beverages but still miss alcohol's euphoria, Atkins said he had an idea, though he emphasized it was "just an experimental notion."

Certain substances have been discussed in medical liter-ature as having the ability to relax people and induce sleep without the addictive qualities of tranquilizers or alcohol. Atkins offers his patients a pill containing L-tryptophan, an amino acid; inositol, a B-family vitamin; calcium; and manganese. Could these ingredients be added to dealcoholized beverages without ruining the beverage's taste? Dr. Atkins wondered.

For several days, I tried two of Dr. Atkins's pills before going to sleep, and although I did not fall asleep any sooner I did sleep an hour longer. Next I mashed the large white pellets into a fine powder. This had a bitter, metallic taste. Despite vigorous mixing, the powder did not dissolve in any of the dealcoholized beverages, but I drank the new mixture and again slept the extra time.

The ingredients could be changed to their liquid states, but it is doubtful that their bitter taste could be masked without putting additives into the dealcoholized beverages. (The recent publicity given to L-tryptophan's sleep-inducing qualities has increased both the demand for it and its price. No side effects have been reported, except for a slightly upset stomach in a very few cases.)

What is clear to Atkins is that the new dealcoholized drinks have great potential. "Combining the desire to drink alcohol and the desire to stay fit create a powerful force," says Atkins.

Problems?

Some people worry about how the wide-spread availability of dealcoholized beverages would affect recovered alcoholics. "The danger is the recovered alcoholic will drink the dealco-holized beer or wine and find he doesn't return to his old behaviors," says Peter B., a member of Alcoholics Anony-mous. "So the recovered alcoholic next tells himself he really can try regular booze. I've been to Switzerland where they have these alcohol-free wines," adds Peter, an international management consultant. "The results were disastrous for recovered alcoholics."

Alcoholism therapy, however, teaches the alcoholic to "surrender rather than comply," to recognize he or she never can drink safely any type of alcoholic beverage. If successful, such treatment protects recovered alcoholics from having to test themselves with the dealcoholized beverages. Recognizing that they need no outside chemical assistance to cope with life, truly recovered alcoholics would not be tempted by these new drinks.

I recently was talking with a recovered alcoholic who is president of a well-known publishing concern. She happened to say, "I've been drinking alcohol-free beer regularly for six years, since I became sober, because I like the taste and there's absolutely no alcohol in it." I explained there was a very small amount, but since it was less than a half a percent the brewer could legally advertise the beverage as alcohol-free. The executive's face froze: "I thought I'd been completely sober, never touched alcohol since treatment."

Now that she knew the beer contained some alcohol and she had experienced no problems, would she continue to drink it? "I don't know. The whole idea six years ago of going to a hospital for counseling and then attending Alcoholics Anonymous was to live completely abstinent. To know anything can set you off. You even avoid certain medicines and salad dressings with alcohol that might start you drinking again if you feel alcohol's effects. I don't know if I'll continue drinking this beer."

Professor Luigi Barbera of Italy's Bologna Medical School recently wrote an enthusiastic memo to clinic staff about dealcoholized wine and argued that it should be prescribed to alcoholics among others: "On one side dealcoholized wine maintains the beneficial properties of wine such as the content of electrolytes, vitamins and essential amino acids. Most important of all, the marketing of a product which keeps the peculiar properties of wine allows an effective prevention of 'alcohol pathology.' This product can be prescribed to all those patients for whom the avoidance of alcoholic beverages represents a severe deprivation from a psychological point of view. The use of dealcoholized wine might (also) be beneficial to patients affected with a documented pattern of metabolic pathology, with liver disease, chronic pancreatitis and also to individuals affected with peptic ulcers."

Those wary of embracing dealcoholized wines and beers, however, emphasize that parents may offer them to their children at dinners and parties. Youth will begin thinking about drinking at earlier ages, and so may experiment with real alcohol sooner.

Already 87 percent of the nation's tenth to twelfth graders report having drunk alcohol. It seems unlikely that dealcoholized beverages would result in a significant drop in the already young age when alcohol is first tried. More importantly, dealcoholized beverages would allow parents to learn that they can drink for taste rather than to alter their mood. This is a crucial step to curbing youthful alcohol abuse. Studies show parental behavior is the major influence in determining the drinking habits of children. The present problem is that 8 percent of the nation's tenth, eleventh, and twelfth graders are already drinking three to four times a week, and 31 percent report being drunk at least six times a year.

The ingredient labels on dealcoholized beverages also may help make people aware that drinking is a health decision. Commenting on the contents information on the Giovane bottle, the company's president, Richard Adlai, said, "I know regular wines don't have this. But we are marketing the beverage to the health conscious. They are concerned with what they put in their bodies so we should tell them the contents. And we expect eventually more and more people to be health aware." The label notes Giovane has per glass thirty-eight calories, 30 percent of the recommended allowance of vitamin C, and is made from "natural Italian wine from which alcohol has been removed to a percentage of less than one-half of 1 percent by volume, pure condensed grape must, carbon dioxide and natural flavors, sorbic acid and potassium meta bisulfite as preservatives."

The wine industry has refused to list ingredients on its bottles. John A. DeLuca, president of the industry's trade association, angrily says that calls for such consumer information are the "most graphic elements" of the "anti-alcohol lobby." If dealcoholized wines with ingredients labels begin to appear next to regular wine bottles in retail stores, they could force wine manufacturers also to reveal their products' contents.

Alcoholic beverages are known to contain congeners or trace residues that remain after production. For example, methanol, commonly used as a solvent and antifreeze, is a more abundant congener in wine than in beer or distilled spirits. Other substances include lead, iron, cobalt, histamines, additives, coloring agents, and tannins. An ingredient label has practical importance because the amount of different congeners varies not only with the type of beverage but also with the brand. Noting this in a study of congener prevalence, Hebe Greizerstein, of New York's Research Institute on Alcoholism, concluded that there is "the need to consider congener effects when assessing health problems." Studies have indicated that heavy wine or beer drinkers — six or more glasses a day — could consume over time a level of congeners that can possibly have negative health effects.

Drinking cheap red wine, as little as two glasses a day, can produce headaches and nausea, according to David Goldberg, a British psychiatrist. Calling this condition "red head" and blaming it on an unknown wine additive, Goldberg told *Alcoholism* magazine, "In the present state of ignorance (of the ingredients), preventive medicine may be the best treatment."

Some alcohol-removed beers reveal their contents, though most regular beers do not. News reports have noted that certain beers contain chemicals to maintain foam and "functional additives" that speed up the brewing process and extend shelf life. Some of these chemicals have been linked to cancer in laboratory animals: 114 of 215 West German beers tested contained dimethylnitrosamine. One 0.5 percent beer, Metbrau, lists as its contents, "a malt beverage containing water, barley, malt hops, gum arabic and papain" (an additive to help the brewing, which the firm claims virtually disappears during the process). In early 1983, a U.S. District Court ordered the Treasury Department to require beer, wine and liquor containers to list their ingredients or carry an address where consumers can write for this information starting in 1984. The court noted that between a half million to 1.7 million people suffer allergies and other health reactions to certain ingredients in alcoholic beverages. The alcohol industry has announced it will appeal.

When?

What is the major restraint on the growth of dealcoholized beverages: The main answer is time. Significant time is required for health warnings, after appearing briefly in the media, to become a matter of public discussion, creating greater media attention and finally measurable changes in behavior.

Decaffeinated coffee was introduced in 1908 but did not capture a sizeable public for nearly seventy years. In particular, reports about caffeine's possible connection to birth defects, pancreatic cancer, and ovarian cysts have caused regular coffee drinkers to switch to decaffeinated brands.

According to a recent Federal Trade Commission report, most Americans are still unaware of the health dangers from smoking despite the Surgeon General's 1964 indictment of cigarettes as cancer causing, yet a gradual but permanent decline in smoking is recognizable. By 1990 Americans are expected to be smoking about 15 percent less, 3,100 cigarettes per person compared to 3,600 in the early 1970s.

And the first federal study on alcohol's health effects was not published until 1980. This report, *Health Hazards Associated with Alcohol,* discusses excessive alcohol's link to cancer of the mouth, liver, and colon as well as vitamin deficiencies and concludes, "numerous information gaps and substantial misinformation relating to alcohol use exist among the American public."

A new product often has unexpected problems that further delay its introduction to the public. An Australian dealcoholized wine producer, which removes alcohol through gentle heating, recently found that the heat and swirling motion aboard ship had produced a refermented wine. It dumped 14,000 bottles rather than pay the stiff U.S. duty and tax of 55 cents a gallon for imported alcoholic beverages.

The process of boiling away alcohol has been known for centuries. Heat disorders a liquid's taste, however, and unlike the Australian company most dealcoholized beverage manufacturers use low pressure to separate out the alcohol. Decreasing the pressure lowers a liquid's boiling point, and as the wine passes through vacuum chambers, the alcohol evaporates off.

While some decaffeinated coffee makers have used a solvent, usually methylene chloride, to remove caffeine, the dealcoholized beverage process of either heat or pressure is a natural one. The pressure-removal method especially avoids the taste complaints associated with decaffeinated coffee. As Michael Sivitz, an expert in coffee technology, says, "Decaffeinated coffees have always been second class in taste and aroma properties. The reasons for this lie in the severe treatment to which the green coffee beans are exposed. The steam wetting, the chlorinated solvent rinsing, and the many hours of steaming to distill off the last residues of solvent tend to destroy the factors that contribute to natural coffee bean aroma and flavor."

While dealcoholized drinks avoid this taste change, they have a distribution problem that the caffeine-free beverages lack. At supermarkets, coffee shoppers will see decaffeinated coffee next to their regular brands, but the 0.5 percent wines and beer, which are legally alcohol-free, are found only in food shops, since liquor stores by law or choice normally sell only alcoholic beverages. In some states, such as New York, new legislation is needed to permit liquor stores to carry dealcoholized beverages. At present, they can sell only wine that is at least 7 percent alcohol.

"This is a touchy change that has to be studied," comments Dr. Robert Cancro, head of psychiatry at New York University–Bellevue Medical Schools. "The first impression is to want the dealcoholized brews prominently displayed in liquor stores. But what if they attract nondrinkers? Will these persons go to the liquor stores to buy the dealcoholized beverages and while there make alcohol purchases, decide to stock up the house, that they normally wouldn't have made? You risk raising overall alcohol consumption."

The restrictions in New York aim at giving uniformity to wine content as well as controlling what supermarkets and liquor stores carry. The former can sell beer while the latter cannot, but liquor stores offer wine while supermarkets are not allowed to. The intent of the New York regulations is also to restrict the number of alcohol outlets. If liquor stores receive the right to sell dealcoholized wines, however, then supermarket owners will press for reciprocal legislation allowing them to sell regular wine.

Low-calorie, low-alcohol beers captured a sizeable public in only fifteen years, dating from the 1960s when the U.S. Brewers Association pointed out that beer drinkers were becoming ready to accept less-filling beverages. Unlike the giant brewers who pushed these new beers, however, the dealcoholized beverage companies are small firms with limited resources to solve their new-product worries.

The major beer and wine producers, who have just started to introduce their lower alcohol and calorie "light" beverages, don't want to confuse the public by advancing another new product. The advertising, research, and lobbying powers of these corporations are not available to push the dealcoholized beverages. The nation's largest wine producer, E. & J. Gallo Winery, told me bluntly, through Daniel Solomon, its communications director, "We are not attempting to market any nonalcoholic wines, either in the United States or in Europe."

Until the attitudes of drinkers can be clearly determined, the 0.5 percent drinks probably will be produced by small firms. It was 25 years after Dr. Ludwig Roselius founded the first firm to make decaffeinated coffee in Germany before General Foods decided this new brew had a potential market and purchased the Sanka brand trademark and U.S. rights (Sanka comes from the French *sans caffeine).*

But while Roselius was motivated to develop decaffeinated coffee after his father, a coffee merchant, died prematurely from what the son thought was too much caffeine, the dealcoholized wine producers are motivated by profits. Richard Adlai, the president of Giovane, explains that the Italian company used to remove alcohol from cheap wine to increase the proof of the brandy it sold. Why not use a better wine grape and also sell the dealcoholized wine, the Italians reasoned. Adlai points out that they chose the name Giovane, which means youth, to capture the new health spirit.

In addition to the pursuit of profits, the adoption of ever tougher drunk-driving laws should spur the small dealcoholized companies to market their liquids. Because of Norway's severe penalties for drunk drivers, in bars people often ask for an Olsen Drink, an alcohol-free gingerale mix, as their last drink(s), reports Stein Berg, who works for an alcoholism education group in that country. Noting Norway's small domestic market, he says the one gingerale manufacturer would have closed if not for this drink's popularity.

In Queens, New York, a bar recently opened that sparked a number of news stories: The Sober Knights serves only nonalcoholic drinks, such as Cranapple Frothy. Owner Walter Jackowski claims "kids" in their early twenties are starting to come to the bar because they enjoy its healthy foods and drinks.

Richard Paul Hinkle, the California wine critic, recently predicted in *Advertising Age* that the "twilight zone" which will see the public regularly use dealcoholized beverages is starting to become visible. "The vast increase in the sales of light beers, diet soft drinks and sparkling mineral waters support the theory that appeals to 'slimness' and 'health' have successful repercussions. It would stand to reason that the combination of these appeals would be an obvious winner. Or ought to be."

Will the calls for a government-led national education campaign to moderate consumption, which the alcohol beverage industry now ridicules as Neo-Prohibition, be seen then as ridiculous by the American public?

Postscript: As with any new product, the buyer may have to try several places before finding dealcoholized beverages. Best bet is the better or "gourmet" food store. Competition for space on the crowded supermarket shelves is intense, and so the dealcoholized beers are rarely found there. Some states permit the dealcoholized wines to be sold in retail liquor stores; however, because of limited space it is unlikely that these stores will carry the alcohol-removed wines.

The addresses of the dealcoholized beverages that I tried follows. This is not an inclusive list of brands.

Castella Wine: Ian Brown, Berkeley, CA 94708.

Giovane Wine: Hilton Commercial Group, 650 West Terrace Drive, San Dimas, CA 91773.

Kingsbury Beer: G. Heileman, 100 Harborview Plaza, La Crosse, WI 54601.

Metbrau Beer: Iroquois Brands, Metropolis Brewery, Trenton, NJ 08611.

Texas Select Beer: Richland Corp., P.O. Box 58024, Dallas, TX 75258.

Just days before this book went to the printer, Hilton Commercial Group sent me ten new dealcoholized wines. The new varieties and my opinion of them are: Carl Jung, from Germany (white, sparkling white, rosé, red) — very good to excellent; Chateau, from Norway (bitter, vermouth, sangria) — poor, tasting too sweet, perfumed; Alive Polarity, from France (white, two reds) — poor to good, tending to be bitter.

3

New Public Policies

In addition to a national campaign to teach new drinking habits, the second major thrust of a drive to help Americans become moderate drinkers would involve significantly increasing alcohol taxes. The question is, are people willing to pay more to stop alcohol from being abused — both by themselves and others?

The cost of alcoholic beverages has increased far less than the prices of other goods. From 1974 to 1979 retail liquor prices rose 14.8 percent in contrast to a 47.2 percent climb in other consumer costs. "Consumer prices of all food products since 1967 [through 1979] advanced almost twice as fast as consumer prices of whiskey," emphasizes the 1980 annual report of the distilled spirits industry.

Higher-tax proponents link this relative price decrease to the rise in worldwide per capita alcohol consumption, which increased 40 percent between 1960 and 1973. Americans increased their drinking by a stiff 25 percent in the 1960s. They have continued to drink more, though in the 1970s the increase slowed to 8 percent.

Small restaurants and bars once gave free hors d'oeuvres in the evening to drinkers. Now their advertisements increasingly offer a free drink or a free second drink with a meal. It is cheaper for the bar drinker or party host to call for or offer an extra round than extra food. A six-pack of beer often costs less than its soft drink equivalent.

After studying how alcohol prices were connected to the

amount of drinking and in turn to drunken highway fatalities and deaths by cirrhosis of the liver, the 1981 report on alcohol use by a National Research Council panel stated, "We conclude that alcohol consumption and the problems caused by it respond to the price of alcoholic beverages, and we infer that the large reductions in the real cost of alcohol to consumers in recent years are likely to have exacerbated drinking problems."

Highly taxed alcohol beverages, the arguments stress, will force the 15 million heavy drinkers, or at least the 5 million of them who are not alcoholic, to drink less. Coupled with the public education campaign, costly alcohol drinks also will reduce the chances that the 85 million nonheavy drinkers might take one(s) too many.

Canada's Addiction Research Foundation has recommended that each year the cost of alcoholic drinks be increased — by taxing alcohol products — by the same percentage as the growth in Canada's after-tax income.

Similarly, the Finnish Parliament has called for increased taxes on all alcohol beverages. In 1981, before the declaration of martial law, Poland raised taxes on high-alcohol content beverages, primarily liquor, to discourage consumption.

A recent Trinidad study showed that when taxes on rum were high, drunk-driving accidents fell, and that highway fatalities jumped when taxes dropped. Dr. Michael Beaubron, a Trinidad psychiatrist, says that if he is given the per capita income and the price of rum for any year he can accurately estimate the number of accidents for that period.

Although the Reagan Administration in 1982 discussed raising alcohol as well as cigarette excise taxes, the amount mentioned was a possible "small tax increase," as a Department of Health and Human Services document stated, since the goal was new revenue rather than boosting prices to discourage consumption. Congress eventually approved, with support of the President, doubling the cigarette tax to sixteen cents a pack effective January, 1983 — without any tax increase for liquor, wine, or beer, demonstrating well the power of the alcohol beverage industry.

Senators rejected a proposal to hike the liquor tax in return for halving the cigarette excise tax. Senator Thomas Eagleton of Missouri said, "The whole world knows beer is the beverage of moderation, it is the mother's milk of American Legion picnics." While the latter may be true, the former is not: beer is the greatest source of alcohol in the nation and the beverage most abused by teenagers.

U.S. officials are reluctant to consider large tax hikes, the 1981 National Research Council study found, primarily because of government's great failure to regulate drinking from 1920 to 1933. Now that Prohibition's shadow is fading, the growing statistics of alcohol abuse are gaining attention, and the proposals calling for stiff taxes to moderate consumption are being raised in other nations, the high-tax strategy should be considered by Washington, the Research Council's panel concluded. Titling its report *Alcohol and Public Policy: Beyond the Shadow of Prohibition,* it called on the nation to escape the ghosts of the past.

The World Health Organization has also recommended that governments go beyond raising alcohol prices just to compensate for inflation. It states, "Manipulation of prices by taxation policies that keep them [alcohol prices] from falling relative to the average price of other commodities has been the minimal recommendation to counter the current increase in consumption, but, clearly, raising the real price of alcohol, rather than preventing it from falling, would be a more effective means of reducing consumption."

Federal excise taxes of about $1.66 on a bottle of liquor and less than 4 cents for a bottle of wine have not been increased since 1951, although the consumer price index rose 238 percent in this time. The beer tax of around 3.6 cents on a pint has not gone up since 1964, while the consumer index rose 183 percent.

The Center for Science in the Public Interest, which is concerned with nutritional health, has called for tripling federal taxes on wine, beer, and liquor to make up for inflation, as well as hiking the rates on the first two to equal those on distilled spirits. The Center estimates that this would produce $25 billion in annual revenues, about the amount the Reagan Administration has cut from health and social services.

Such an increase would raise the price of the average $7.50 bottle of liquor by about 44 percent, to $10.80. Equal tax rates, based on the amount of alcohol in each drink, mean a twelve-ounce, 50-cent can of beer would jump to about 77 cents, a hike of 54 percent, and a $5.00 bottle of wine would go to around $6.50, a 30 percent rise. Per drink costs would rise even more since bars mark up tax increases to customers.

To what extent will price increases reduce excessive consumption in the United States? The answer is difficult to estimate and has to be based on the experience of states, whose tax rises, though small, have been more frequent than those of the federal government or on the example of other nations, where income levels and cultures may be very different. Philip Cook of the Institute for Public Policy Studies at Duke University suggests an elasticity of increased price to decreased consumption of -1.0 or less; the liquor industry guesses at -.5; workers in the Treasury Department predict between -1.0 to -.3. These estimated rates mean a boost in the retail cost of a certain alcoholic beverage by 30 percent could drop its consumption level by 30, 15, or 9 percent.

Opponents of high taxes argue that Americans have not significantly reduced their driving despite the sharp increase in gas prices. Supporters respond by pointing to the drop in meat sales, which is blamed on the combination of large cost increases and increased health awareness about fatty foods.

Dr. Morris Chafetz, the first head of the government's National Institute on Alcohol Abuse and Alcoholism, argues: "A higher excise tax won't price alcoholic people out of the market; the illness compels them to drink. The persons an excise tax will price out of the market are those who can take alcohol or leave it." High prices, however, are not meant to affect the alcoholic, but rather the heavy and average drinkers who "can take it or leave it."

Dr. Gail Allen, director of the alcoholism treatment program at St. Luke's Hospital in New York and a member of the National Research Council's panel, says: "We all didn't agree completely about the studies we looked at from here and abroad, what their effects would be. They can be interpreted in different ways. But we finally agreed that the links to possibly reducing alcohol problems are too strong for our government to not truly start to consider enacting regulations to control consumption, including a price policy."

One problem is that America is a high-income nation enjoying wide drinking alternatives. In 1980, the retail price for a bottle of a well-known brand of liquor ranged between $10.37 (Dewar's Scotch) and $5.65 (Seagram's Gin), a nearly 90 percent fluctuation. There are also far cheaper beers and wines available. Does the public, and in turn politicians, fear that a tax policy to eliminate excessive drinking could lead to repeated price increases until great numbers of people were unable to afford a drink? This would open the way for the illegal manufacture and bootlegging whose corruption spread so easily during Prohibition.

The *U.S. Journal,* a newspaper in the alcohol abuse field, argues that to significantly reduce excessive consumption will require a retail price boost of 200 percent. A 1977 report from the British House of Commons warned, "We do not recommend, for example, that alcoholic drinks should, by the increase of taxation, be priced out of the reach of many people."

A too-high tax also could force those most dependent on alcohol as a relaxant into using other and now very available mood-altering drugs, such as amphetamines, barbiturates, and marijuana. Taken excessively, these can cause fatal accidents and serious health damage. Also, studies in which average drinkers were denied alcoholic beverages resulted in their later giving these beverages an especially high taste rating, indicating that certain restrictions can backfire.

But if reasonably higher prices — just to keep pace with inflation, for example — could decrease consumption, to what extent would alcohol abuse problems be lowered? "There is good evidence from econometric studies that alcohol prices, as affected by excise taxation, can affect consumption levels, and

New Public Policies   47

probably the consequent rates of alcohol-related problems," the Research Council's study group concludes.

Professor Cook of Duke University says his statistical studies show that even small price boosts will affect alcohol abuse. For every 1 percent increase in retail price, auto deaths would fall by .7 percent and deaths by cirrhosis of the liver by .9 percent. Based on these figures, a 25 percent decrease in the nation's alcohol-related highway fatalities would require a 35 percent price increase. Can legislators be convinced that a major hike in consumer prices, resulting from a significant increase in the alcohol excise tax, should be approved?

"The pattern of use — one drug or a mixture of two — is not inherent in their chemical molecules but is determined by a host of legal, social, psychological, and economic factors," remarks the Consumers Union in its national survey, *Licit and Illicit Drugs.* Proponents declare that *combined* with an education campaign against any form of chemical abuse, high taxes would lead people away from alcohol and to less costly and less harmful, or more treatable, habits. "If we eliminate actual drugs from our consideration," writes Leslie Farber, the social critic, "the addictive possibilities are endless: cigarettes, chocolate, detective and spy stories, football on television, psychoanalysis." Large coffee urns and overflowing ashtrays mark Alcoholics Anonymous meetings. While the drunk can kill himself and others on any day, caffeine and nicotine addictions are slower in creating their damage, and so there is more time to get help for an individual.

Supporters admit that any big alcohol tax increase will be regressive, taking a disproportionate amount of money from the budgets of poor families. They justify this by noting that alcoholic beverages are luxury items and as such should be taxed more severely while perhaps lowering taxes that affect basic household commodities. Low-income drinkers could gain indirectly from a high tax that discourages consumption, argues the National Research Council panel, since they are the least able to pay for the health damage and personal financial loss associated with alcohol abuse. The report recommends government using part of the increase in alcohol tax revenues as "additions to minimum income maintenance programs."

Despite these arguments, the discrimination charge disturbs many high-tax advocates. They can visualize headlines declaring that while many Americans now drink less, the wealthy are unaffected as well as headlines proclaiming dramatic reductions in fatal accidents and disorderly violence. Costly alcohol may reduce the harm caused by alcohol but increase the damage that results from another advertisement of America as an inequitable society.

William Raspberry, a *Washington Post* writer who is black, has endorsed the high-tax policy as a necessary choice. "Even those of us who would like to see Reagan change his mind about his mammoth defense outlays, or who favor the closing of some of the more unconscionable tax loopholes for the rich, can see the value of a proposal that promises to improve both the physical and fiscal health of the nation."

Opponents of government efforts to reduce how much people drink point to *1984* and its Big Brother warning about government interference in private behaviors. Orwell's novel, however, also talks about a society where the cost of all goods — except liquor — keeps rising beyond the budgets of people and drinking is encouraged to forget this: "There had never been quite enough to eat, one had never had socks or underclothes that were not full of holes, furniture had always been battered and rickety, rooms underheated, tube trains crowded, houses falling to pieces, bread dark-colored, tea a rarity, coffee filthy-tasting, cigarettes insufficient — nothing cheap and plentiful except synthetic gin."

The defenders of government policies to control consumption argue that the decision to increase prices should be given the go-ahead because the potential good dramatically overwhelms any potential problems. This conclusion assumes that permanently lowered drinking levels would lead to large health improvements.

Canada, Finland, Norway, and the United States, all countries which once had and repealed prohibition, enjoyed during their chaotic but dry periods the lowest levels ever of alcohol-related deaths and accidents. Before the nation approved Prohibition, Michigan passed its own law in 1917. In his book *Intemperance,* Larry Englemann reproduces the statistics published in the *Detroit News* in 1918 comparing what happened in the now-dry city to the previous year's experiences:

	Wet	Dry
Accidents	5993	4950
Attempted suicides	90	49
Suicides	67	45
Dead bodies found on the streets	77	35
Felonious assaults	361	152
Homicides	78	38
Robberies	775	295
Drunkenness	7290	3624
Nonsupport cases	767	452
Vagrancy	332	49
Automobile accidents	96	68
Death from alcoholism	92	17

Finland provides more recent experiences about the effects of alcohol controls (or lack of them). In 1972, employees in the ALKO stores, the state-controlled alcohol retail shops which sell half of all alcoholic beverages, went on strike for a month. The result was a marked decrease in arrests for public drunkenness and drunk driving as well as alcohol-caused hospital admissions. The Finnish Parliament is now considering legislation to limit consumption through raising alcohol taxes to match the growth in income and requiring business people — as a form of social pressure — to separate out on their entertainment deductions for income taxes the amount spent for alcohol in restaurants.

As the World Health Organization notes: "Underlying the

current policies in a number of countries is the consideration that alcoholic beverages should be made available to meet the 'legitimate' demands of populations, but that restrictions should be introduced to limit the possible harmful effects of consumption."

U.S. consumers will not accept large price changes, argues Frederick Meister, president of the liquor industry's trade association. "It is not sound tax policy to penalize the majority of alcohol consumers for the excesses of a few or the infrequent excesses of the majority."

The findings of a poll led by Michael Goodstadt of a representative group of Ontario's population present another view: two-thirds of all drinkers there would pay more "if the long-term result would be a decrease in the prevalence of alcoholism." Of the price increase supporters, primarily women and light drinkers, more than half said they would pay up to two dollars more for a bottle of liquor or wine or twelve bottles of beer. The 1982 Gallup survey also found support for a price increase: 54 percent of Americans supported doubling the taxes on liquor, and 49 percent favored this 100 percent increase for beer and wine. College graduates (65 percent) and women (59 percent) were the strongest higher-tax advocates (see Appendix B).

As the government already is spending personal income taxes on alcohol abuse's consequences, the average person will gain by beverage tax hikes that decrease consumption and the harmful effects of alcohol. Treatment costs far exceed the extra tax dollars that alcohol consumers will pay. This argument was stressed recently by California voters in a thus far unsuccessful fight for a beverage tax to fund alcohol treatment and prevention efforts. The California group emphasized that price rises are onerous only to the heaviest drinkers. Its public call declared, "The people of California find that alcohol-related problems and alcoholism are an increasingly costly burden on the personal lives and pocketbooks of California citizens; that a small minority of the population consumes the vast majority of alcoholic beverages sold. . ."

When?

Until the general public becomes aware enough of the new proposals to limit consumption and begins debating them in the media, the present professional reports supporting this moderation thrust "will gather dust on a policy-maker's desk," observes Michael Jacobson of Washington's Center for Science in the Public Interest.

At a recent meeting of a half-dozen directors of New York City health institutions, the question of boosting alcohol taxes to discourage high consumption was discussed. Several persons immediately expressed support, but others said they were unsure because of the regressive effects on the poor. They also worried about being labeled "extremists," noted Dr. Jay Goldsmith, head of this committee and executive director of the Jewish Board of Family and Children's Services, one of the largest nonprofit health agencies in the country. "Promoting sharp changes whose effects are not completely known can hurt our credibility with people in government and the private sector," Goldsmith said, "even if we personally favor these reforms."

His group decided not to vote, but instead recommended seminars for New York's health workers about government policies to limit excessive consumption. Once aware of the views among city health professionals, this committee and others like it could prepare a statement and release it to the press. An endorsement by these leaders would help bring the issue to the public's attention.

Disseminating information from the alcohol field to other health sectors and then waiting for the media to pick up on this and for public opinion to form and express itself is a slow process. However, supporters of moderate-drinking efforts appear to have no other choice. Government officials will not readily launch a strong national campaign of the kind so far discussed involving values against drunkenness and high taxes since such a move has anti-individual rights, anti-consumer, and anti-poor liabilities. The *U.S. Journal,* the alcohol and drug newspaper, asks, "At a time when such massive efforts are being undertaken to hold down the consumer price index, who is going to come out and advocate price increases that go beyond increased production, distribution or marketing costs?"

Since they are still just proposals, these approaches to reducing alcohol consumption lack the "hard news" angle that daily newspapers require in their stories. Because of the far-ranging social changes they can produce, however, these policies are appropriate topics for TV and magazine coverage. Will these media resist, consciously or unconsciously, giving major time or space to this issue because of the great alcohol advertising revenue they receive?

In 1979, for example, liquor companies accounted for 16.3 percent of the ad revenue of *Newsweek,* 11.6 percent of *Time,* and 14 percent of *U.S. News & World Report.* In addition to this space, the magazines also carried wine and beer ads. Unlike liquor, beer (and wine) can be advertised on TV as well as in the print media. In 1979, the beer industry spent $368.9 million in advertising, with 92.3 percent of the ads concentrated in the broadcast media.

Ogilvy & Mather, one of the nation's largest advertising agencies, recently prepared a magazine public service ad on teenage drinking. Its lengthy message discussed the reasons for teenagers to limit their drinking. The ad emphasized that "alcohol is a drug," that it was easy to lose self-control when drinking, and that the choice of how much to drink was a significant one. In contrast to other magazine ads on alcohol abuse — which carry the general theme of "drink responsibly" or deal with alcoholism rather than the habits of all American drinkers — this long, 350-word ad discussed specifically that alcohol should be enjoyed with meals and at social occasions but not alone, advised teenagers not to have more than two drinks at any party, and offered other ideas to control consumption. Teenagers who reviewed the ad in a field test replied that they wanted this "straight talk."

An Ogilvy & Mather executive asked two of the nation's largest magazines to run the ad as a public service. He was privately told that the theme was too "controversial" because it could offend alcohol beverage advertisers by discussing ways to permanently cut down on drinking (instead of only before driving or on the New Year's Eve and Memorial Day holidays). After seeing the Ogilvy & Mather ad on teenage drinking, an executive of a magazine and TV organization confided that the ad would never be used by the largest publications since it directly opposed what alcohol advertisers would want to achieve — selling more alcohol.

In a study of *Alcohol and Mass Media*, Dr. Howard Blane, professor of education and psychology at the University of Pittsburgh, quotes from a report to alcohol manufacturers by the Brand Rating Index, which supplies consumer information to advertisers: "Purely and simply, heavy users are the most important customers you have. They are the men who consume well beyond the average . . . The men who account for a markedly disproportionate share of product purchases and usages."

Robert Hammond, executive director of the Alcohol Information Service, writes:

> Now, what if that ideal of "moderation" would be achieved . . . First, consider the total who are of legal age for alcohol consumption, 157.5 million. (Surely the liquor industry would not want those under the legal age to imbibe!) Subtract the abstainers (33 percent) and you are left with 105.5 million legal drinkers. If each were to consume the upper limits of the NIAAA's definition of moderation [0.99 ounces or two drinks per day], that would mean a whopping 40 percent decrease in the sale of beer, wine and distilled spirits, based on 1981 sales figures.

A sales executive with CBS Publications confided he would never use the teenage drinking limits ad in any of his magazines that carried alcohol beverage advertisements out of fear of losing this business. A former executive with *Esquire* volunteered to call friends at major publications about using this ad. He was turned down by all that sold space to the big-spending wine, liquor, and beer companies.

The new proposals to limit alcohol consumption and problems will probably reach the public slowly. They will be discussed briefly in those magazines and TV shows that carry little or no alcohol advertising, creating some controversy there, and in notices in newspapers, gradually attracting national media attention. "It is often a source of wonder and consternation for the powers that preside over the great opinion-making organs of our society — in government, in culture and in the media — to discover that the views so fluently disseminated by their vast enterprises have had their origin, more often than not, in the ideas and controversies of obscure intellectual coteries that seemed at the time of their eminence to exist at a great distance from any sort of power or influence," commented Hilton Kramer, the New York Times's former art critic, about one way that ideas reach public attention.

Initially legislators can be expected to avoid the moderate consumption proposals because they involve taking on the alcohol beverage industry, a heavy campaign contributor. Wilbur Mills, the former Congressional leader and a recovered alcoholic, flew to Maine on April 23, 1981, to testify on behalf of proposed legislation for a small state tax to finance alcoholism programs. Designed to raise $3 million yearly for treatment efforts, this special-purpose tax was similar to those already passed by twenty-three states, and would, at five cents a gallon for beer, fourteen cents a gallon for wine, and sixty-two and one half cents a gallon for liquor, increase the cost to the drinker about "one-half cent a drink," says Dick Loomer, executive director of the Maine Council on Alcoholism. "This tax obviously had no link to lowering consumption." After its approval Governor Joseph Brennan said, "this was the most important piece of human service legislation" he had signed.

Arriving at the Maine airport, Mills was greeted by messages from alcohol industry lobbyists that asked him not to speak. He returned one phone call and was told that his law firm would lose a beer industry client if he testified. Mills confided this remark to those with him, and then went to Augusta to give his testimony.

"This legislation, involving such a small amount of money, required a great amount of time to get it to the attention of the public and the lawmakers," says Loomer. "The alcohol industry had to be taken on. With respect to the success we had in fighting the industry, it was done through the people of the state. We solicited the support of every possible organization within the state of Maine and through those organizations got to the grass roots."

Diana Tabler, who was director of the National Council on Alcoholism's public policy office in Washington, D.C., tells about a director of alcoholism services for a southern state who proposed a small increased tax on beer. Suddenly his department was audited by five different outside state agencies. The director learned that lobbyists from the alcohol beverage manufacturers had contacted legislators, who in turn requested that his department be audited. The director, appointed by the governor, wanted to stop this harassment which threatened to shut down his agency's work as well as create bad publicity. He dropped this tax increase idea.

Bob Woods is helping to organize the California coalition that wants to place on the ballot a referendum to increase taxes on alcohol beverages by about five cents a drink and raise $650 million. He admits that he does not know if he can beat the strong opposition from the beverage companies. "The industry does not want to see its products tied directly to alcohol-related problems."

Considering the alcohol business's strong opposition to these small taxes whose effect on the consumer would be at most pennies and so not discourage consumption, the proposals to actually moderate America's drinking through higher taxes and national drinker-awareness projects can expect powerful resistance once they fully enter the public arena.

Frederick Meister, the liquor industry association's head,

discussed the power of his members by noting that their tax contributions to government would "cover the total federal spending for housing and urban renewal plus the costs of the U.S. air transportation system plus pay the federal share of 1.7 billion school lunches." Meister has threatened that a 10 percent drop in alcohol consumption would cost the federal government $600 million in taxes and the states $500 million.

Other Proposals to Moderate Drinking

Despite the industry's threats the proposals for an educational campaign and an increased alcohol tax continue to gain supporters within the health field, and other measures are being considered as well. Congressional hearings in 1976, for example, discussed the possibility of banning wine and beer as well as liquor commercials from TV screens (a step called for in Canada by the Canadian Medical Association). At the end of 1982, four former top government officials called for the "reexamination" of the marketing and advertising of alcoholic beverages and suggested ultimately eliminating all alcohol commercials from TV. They stated that "the massive amount of advertising ($1 billion yearly) can only increase alcohol consumption and the inevitable consequences. As a first step, we urge that the voluntary ban on broadcast liquor advertising be extended to beer and wine." The officials were William Hathaway, former chairman of the Senate Subcommittee on Alcoholism and Drug Abuse; Nicholas Johnson, former commissioner of the Federal Communications Commission; and Dr. Ernest Noble and John R. DeLuca, the directors of the National Institute on Alcohol Abuse and Alcoholism under Presidents Ford and Carter. (John R. DeLuca is not related to John A. DeLuca, head of the Wine Institute.)

Since Marx and Lenin blamed alcohol abuse on capitalist advertising that pressured people to drink too much, the Soviet Union and most Eastern European countries have outlawed alcohol ads. Yet their drunkenness problems remain, emphasize opponents of advertising restrictions. In 1976, Hungary outlawed alcohol advertising *and* placed a 25 percent excise tax on distilled spirits. Reports since that time indicate a 20 percent decline in per capita alcohol consumption.

Another proposal aimed at moderating consumption recommends labeling liquor, wine, and beer bottles with warnings that alcohol is dangerous when taken with pills, when abused by pregnant women, and when consumed before driving. In 1979, the Senate passed legislation requiring warning labels on liquor bottles: "Caution: consumption of alcoholic beverages may be hazardous to your health." The House did not pass a companion bill, however. To deter further action, the liquor, wine, and beer companies volunteered to conduct public awareness campaigns about abusive drinking's link to birth defects. The Treasury Department has stated it will evaluate the effects of this limited effort, and the label question remains an open one (see Chapter 8).

This issue has attracted public attention. Virginia Schneider of Springfield, Illinois, wrote about labels in the following letter to the editor of *Alcoholism:* "If only my late husband had been warned in time (that) the excessive amount of whiskey he drank for years would literally eat away his esophagus through cancer, he might still be here today . . . I sure miss him. His children do too. We wish, oh how we wish, he were still here with us. We need him so." In contrast, the National Council on Drugs, with such responsible members as the American Dental Association and American Medical Association, has opposed labels, noting that "experience has demonstrated that warning labels have been largely ineffective."

Opponents of bottle warnings want to kill this question rather than debate it. In 1982, the National Council on Alcoholism, the leading voluntary group concerned with alcoholism, advocated warning labels as well as higher taxes and advertising restrictions for the first time since its founding. Philip Morris, owner of Miller Beer, subsequently notified the New York chapter that it would not contribute to the agency's annual dinner, the proceeds from which support counseling services for alcoholics. The refusal letter specifically mentioned as its reason the parent organization's new policy positions.

The alcohol beverage industry has even accused the staff of the National Institute on Alcohol Abuse and Alcoholism of secretly being behind the labeling and control of consumption ideas. "Our own NIAAA when you scratch below the surface is, you might say, Neo-Prohibitionist," accuses Dr. Thomas Turner, medical director of the U.S. Brewers Association. When President Carter appointed John DeLuca head of the NIAAA, the director was immediately told by the wine industry's California-based trade association that if he pursued the labeling issue his department's "funding would be in jeopardy."

The NIAAA's position on alcohol abuse prevention, presented in its popular pamphlet *Facts About Alcohol and Alcoholism,* is far from being rash or temperance-minded, as the beverage industry infers by use of the Neo-Prohibitionist tag. The booklet concludes: "Perhaps the most difficult prevention approach is to change the cultural significance of drinking. Sanctions on drinking exercise a great influence over the individual drinker and establish a status quo within the community. Thus, introduction of healthy drinking attitudes could go far to influence individual and group drinking patterns and behaviors."

An eighteen-nation seminar sponsored by ANSVAR, the Swedish insurance conglomerate that focuses its sales on nondrinkers, found that although India was now the only country requiring a bottle warning, eleven countries expected to have such a law in the next five years. The danger, participants noted, was that this legislation was relatively easy to pass since it placed no financial burden on either the consumer or alcohol-beverage industry and allowed governments to declare they had attacked alcohol abuse. The public might expect a significant drop in alcohol-related problems, except it would not occur. The seminar concluded that people need to realize the obvious: it is not easy for an individual to change a long-held habit. This difficulty becomes formidable when a nation attempts to adopt a new behavior. *All* the fiscal, regulatory, and educational proposals to moderate consumption are needed if they are to succeed.

One participant, Klaus Makela, pointed to a new law in Finland that placed penalties on anyone who gives alcohol to a minor. This legislation has "no practical significance," emphasized Makela, avoids "the responsibility for economic consequences of some restrictive policies," and misleads the public into believing that government has acted meaningfully.

The 1982 Gallup survey found that although 61 percent of the respondents wanted a calorie and ingredients label and 54 percent favored doubling the taxes on liquor, only about one-fourth believed that these changes alone would reduce consumption.

Beyond Alcohol

The attempts to regulate alcohol use relate closely to efforts to increase taxes on cigarettes, highly sugared products, foods filled with additives and preservatives, and other goods associated with health and social problems. Restricting alcohol advertising coincides with the arguments to limit TV commercials aimed at youth, because this age group is especially susceptible to these messages.

Efforts to moderate consumption eventually could combine with such nonalcohol issues as well; and if this happens, history will be repeating itself. Sensing it could lead a great spirit of change, the Prohibition Party in the 1890s not only fought to outlaw drinking but also advocated a strongly populist platform, including support of income tax and free trade, abolition of convict labor, woman's suffrage, a day off each week, government ownership of railroads and utilities, government issue of money, and land grants only to actual settlers. The party, however, eventually rejected these calls for broad leadership in favor of a one-theme cause.

Prohibition and the new proposals to control consumption also share a similarity in timing. The political leaders during the Depression championed Prohibition's 1933 repeal in part to demonstrate that new times truly were coming. Now the nation is mired in one of its worst periods of recession and unemployment. If the calls to create a healthier, moderate-drinking nation are put into effect, drinking could again serve as a way to help create a new spirit, a sense that changes are possible.

If supporters of moderate consumption become organized, they will want to avoid confusion with the Moral Majority (which also opposes excessive consumption) as well as to escape the pejorative Neo-Prohibition tag of the alcohol manufacturers. Advocates can explain that unlike the stance of the Moral Majority, the moderate consumption calls are based on studies of alcohol abuse rather than interpretations of morality. They might also attach a common label to their suggestions: a name such as New Health, for example, would attract the attention of many persons who normally have no interest in alcohol abuse but whose involvement is necessary if a public debate is to spread.

Michael Jacobson, of the Center for Science in the Public Interest, whose concerns are foods, diets, and vitamins, has placed his organization behind the reduced-consumption calls. "Now, don't get me wrong," he says. "I am not advocating Prohibition. I like my glass of chablis as much as the next fellow. But thousands of lives and $100 billion a year (his estimate of alcohol abuse's cost to society) is nothing to sneeze at. It is about time society put some real money and muscle into the fight against excessive drinking."

Two years ago, I lectured about alcohol abuse in Israel. As the expert, I tried to relax that country's professionals and explained that Israel had few alcoholics, numbering about seven thousand (less than .2 percent of the population), while the United States measured its alcoholism problem at 5 percent of its citizens, or 10 million persons.

An Israeli official rose and lectured: America is a rich, big country with 220 million people. Perhaps Americans have the strength and wealth not to worry that their alcohol problems keep growing. But Israel, with less than 4 million people and at war, can't tolerate this attitude. If even a thousand youths drop out from society, can't contribute to or defend their country, then Israel has a problem it *must* solve. So, the judge said, please lecture.

America's recognition that it is no longer a land of unlimited resources provides a strong impetus not to tolerate problems that harm it, in both human and financial terms, and that have solutions. This sense could well focus on government measures to solve perhaps the most visible and costly of all social ills —alcohol abuse.

4

A Cure for Drunkenness?

"Scientists have, in large measure, become the determinants of the quality of life in society," wrote Albert Szent-Györgi, the Nobel laureate for medicine. "More history is made at present in laboratories than in national capitals."

Science as well as government has a role in solving the problems of alcohol abuse. The research attempting to eliminate the problem of excessive consumption has adopted an appropriately historical name for its goal: "the amethystic."

This word was coined about ten years ago by Dr. Ernest Noble, a medical researcher at the University of California at Los Angeles, as the label for a chemical that could safely eliminate the effects of intoxication. He derived the amethystic label from the ancient Greeks, who believed that by wearing a violet amethyst around the neck someone could drink alcohol without fear of becoming drunk.

Present amethystic research, led by Noble, who served under President Gerald Ford as director of the National Institute on Alcohol Abuse and Alcoholism, aims at developing a pill that would counteract the disorientation, poor vision, lack of coordination, and aggressiveness that accompany intoxication. Such a pill would "immediately prevent 25,000 deaths each year, half of all fatal highway accidents, and stop the deaths in emergency rooms of people who overdose on alcohol," says Noble. Drunkenness also plays a major role in 69 percent of drownings, 83 percent of deaths in accidental home fires, 86 percent of murders, 50 percent of rapes, and 72 percent of robberies, according to the U.S. Department of Health and Human Services. This costs the United States about $8.5 billion a year, or 17 percent of the nearly $50 billion combined price tag for alcoholism and alcohol abuse.

"I drink, and under proper circumstances I enjoy it," says Noble. "Used moderately, alcohol helps me to relax and relieves stress." The purpose of the amethystic pill, Noble emphasizes, would be to counteract the effects of acute alcohol intoxication, "sufficient to restore the individual's behavior to predrinking levels."

The search for an amethystic is focusing on finding a chemical capable of arousing the brain's catecholamine system, which is involved in the body's fight and flight reactions, and can send a rush of adrenalin into the blood. The ideal chemical manipulation would stimulate the intoxicated person in the same way that a police car's revolving red light in the rear view mirror suddenly affects the drunk driver. A momentary surge of adrenalin hits him, allowing his body to temporarily overcome alcohol's noticeable effects on his thinking and movements.

It is believed that alcohol depletes or blocks the functioning of the catecholamine system, and researchers think that stimulating adrenalin production would allow the body to fight intoxication. Many chemicals can create this stimulation. Researchers seek one that can be taken easily as a pill or liquid that will work within fifteen minutes, remain in the blood long enough to reduce alcohol's effects, create no adverse reactions, such as preventing sleep, and have a low potential to become an abused drug itself.

Present amethystic research has explored and eliminated, as the practical agent, caffeine, various vitamins, and amphetamines, but, according to Noble, "a good deal of success has been achieved most recently with ephedrine, found in drugs for asthma, and with L-dopa, used in Parkinson's disease treatment." He is also testing the arousal effects of brain peptides as well as naloxone, which is used in treating narcotic addicts. "We're almost there," says Noble. "Within ten to fifteen years we'll have the pill or liquid that'll be taken routinely by people who believe they have had too much to drink."

Scientific literature discusses the amethystic's development in matter-of-fact terms, but many people dismiss the pill as a fantasy. Their views change, however, as they learn about the present work and realize that someone like Noble, a leading researcher and the nation's former top official for alcohol abuse, attaches his name to the statement that a sober-up pill could be in regular use within a decade. Public awareness of the amethystic possibilities is especially important since society will shape the role that the anti-intoxicant will play.

Widespread Use Foreseen

Ira Cisin of the Social Research Group at George Washington University, whose report on American drinking practices is considered a landmark in the field of alcohol studies, foresees widespread acceptance of a sober-up pill. "I wouldn't worry too much about the problem of compliance," he says, believing that a sobering pill would be used routinely by those about to drive after drinking. An undesirable side effect — increased drinking — might occur, but despite this the prospect for an anti-drunkenness pill is bright, says Cisin, observing that "even if it worked on only a small proportion of the problem, and even if it didn't work too well, we'd be ahead of where we are now."

Drunk-driving laws also could boost the use of an anti-intoxicant pill. Legislation requiring stiff prison sentences and permanent license revocation for intoxicated drivers is continually proposed in state legislatures. Even though traffic accidents are the greatest cause of violent death in America, there is opposition to such extreme laws. Many argue that a lot of these drivers had no alternative way to travel after they drank. This resistance to strict sanctions would disappear with the prominent placement of a bowl of amethystic capsules next to the bowls of pretzels in bars and homes, offering the drinker a way to become sober before driving.

The specter of a negligence suit may help to guarantee that such bowls become standard objects. There are current laws that allow a person injured by an intoxicated driver to sue the bar owner or party host for negligently continuing to serve someone who has become obviously drunk. The difficulty of proving noticeable intoxication has limited these cases, especially those involving private functions. By the end of the 1980s, juries may need only the answer to one simple question: Did the defendant — bar or individual — provide an adequate supply of amethystic pills that night?

When lawsuits have succeeded in this area, the settlements have been very large. A seventy-five-year-old man from Florida, Douglas Morrison, who was permanently paralyzed after a drunken crash in which he was the driver, recently won $1.2 million from a bar. While there he drank more than a dozen beers at a cost of $34. The barkeeper served him while he was obviously drunk, the jury agreed.

Attorney Harry Lipsig, a fellow of the International Academy of Trial Lawyers, has noted that at present, "courts feel too many problems of proof would arise in establishing the liability of a social host" who serves a drunk guest. Despite this problem, Lipsig believes the state laws against serving someone who appears intoxicated — often called the Dram Shop Act — should be broadly interpreted to place liability on private party givers. "When a social host furnishes liquor to an obviously intoxicated person, there exists a reasonably forseeable risk of harm to others."

Lipsig's arguments have attracted a lot of attention in the legal community but have not yet succeeded in expanding the scope of these negligence laws. One attorney, James F. Oliviero, who successfully defended an employer who held a large Christmas party after which an intoxicated employee was involved in an accident, defended a restricted legal interpretation: "The ability of a host to control the drinking of all guests would be questioned by anyone who has attended such a gathering."

The sober-up pill would offer the party giver a visible way to try to protect society from any drunken guests. The Dram Shop Laws could extend liability to social hosts, who will then have to provide the bowl of amethystics at their gatherings to avoid the possibility of being found negligent.

The growing sales of hand-held, personal breathalyzers is bringing competing models to the public and dropping their price (about $75 at present). The future might see guests testing themselves and if alcohol positive requesting an amethystic pill from hosts. "Test your ability to drive home after the party or game," advertises ALCO. A competitor, ATC, claims it "is the new way to protect you and your loved ones from the devastating consequences of driving under the influence of alcohol."

Availability of an anti-intoxicant pill would also help to reduce crime. A major problem in American society is a return to excessive drinking by released prisoners, coupled with the fact that "83 percent of offenders in prison or jail have reported alcohol involvement in their crimes," according to the National Institute on Alcohol Abuse and Alcoholism. Judges could require certain criminals, when released from jail or freed on probation, to take an anti-intoxicant whenever they drink. If subsequently arrested while drunk, the offender could be quickly jailed for violating the amethystic requirement in their probation or parole orders, instead of being left on the streets awaiting trial for the new offense. The amethystic could not only prevent crime but also unjam the criminal courts.

Considering the heavy economic burden of intoxication — $5.14 billion for motor vehicle accidents, $2.86 billion for crimes, and $.5 billion for fire losses — the federal government also can be expected to become one of the amethystic's chief "pushers."

For the 10 million Americans who are alcoholics, however, the amethystic could be a deadly pill. The chemical would mask intoxication's effects and greatly diminish the chances of identifying alcoholics. As drinking continued, alcoholism's physical damage to the liver, heart, pancreas, and esophagus would intensify. An amethystic is definitely needed, says Anne Geller, a neurologist directing the alcoholism treatment program at St. Luke's-Roosevelt Hospital in New York, but the pill could create a future with "more and more alcoholics finally entering treatment only because of end-organ damage." The only way to "protect" alcoholics may be to make sure that their addiction is treated at the earliest stage — before the alcoholic ever drinks (and the next two chapters discuss this possibility).

Ernest Noble has become affiliated with other efforts to create an antidote to excessive alcohol use. Recently, he was named chairman of the scientific advisory board of Zoe Products, a Los Angeles firm that has put together its own product, "Sober-Aid," which will be available to the public within a year. "This powder did not come out of my work, which is still going on," said Noble. "Zoe Products is not sure where or how it affects the body, but it does seem to work. The powder is made of all natural substances: amino acids, vitamins, sugar, and salts. I can't tell you the exact ingredients because they're still a trade secret. But I can assure you none are toxic." About Sober-Aid, Noble cautions, "If it doesn't eliminate intoxication, it at least can supply the nutrients a heavy drinker loses."

The Food and Drug Administration, however, has issued a statement that Sober-Aid and two similar products — Sober-Up Time from California, and Sober-Up! of Utah — are new drugs requiring agency approval, and that they lack "adequate and well-controlled scientific studies."

Noble recognizes the FDA's charge about the lack of evidence, and says, "My basic scientific research on the amethystic continues. I am confident it will be available within a decade."

5

Compulsory Treatment:
New Help for the Alcoholic

Please help. I just came home and he's out on the floor. The door is open. The baby could've walked away, got hurt. Our apartment is by the stairs. Please, he's done this before.
I'll give you the phone numbers of a hospital clinic and AA.
He won't go. I've tried so many times.
Then why'd you call our alcoholism referral number?
Because he has to go! I thought you'd think of a way. Force him into help right now!
I'm sorry . . .
You're sorry!

That telephone conversation was real. Its frustrated caller was unfortunately too typical of the people who are desperate to get help for the alcoholic, and desperate for themselves.

Now there is new hope for them. The government interventions to promote moderate drinking represent just one aspect of the change in the public's ability to greatly reduce its alcohol problems. A second thrust is aimed at helping Americans control the other part of their alcohol problem: alcoholism.

An alcoholic is the drinker who continually abuses alcohol. Excess consumption is not linked to a special occasion but rather to his or her ability to function daily. Ethanol is a drug, and alcoholics may become physically addicted to it. The body experiences tolerance, the need over time for more alcohol in order to feel its effects. All alcoholics become psychologically and often physically addicted; they depend on the drug and its euphoria to relieve stress and to get them through each day. Being anesthetized also allows alcoholics not to feel guilty for their drunken behavior. The addiction feeds on itself.

Like any addict, the alcoholic cannot give up his drug easily. Only 15 percent of America's 10 million alcoholics go for treatment each year. Their fatal illness remains unchecked. It is one of the nation's major health problems, after cancer and heart disease. Alcoholism affects the lives of another 30 million people, the spouses, children, and relatives of alcoholics. Alcoholism and alcohol abuse cost the nation nearly $50 billion a year, according to NIAAA studies.

Traditional thinking believed there was no way to break this cycle. The alcoholic could be treated successfully only when he wanted help; he had to hit his "bottom" first, be truly suffering.

There has been a revolutionary change in this belief, and it has led to government passing laws to push great numbers of alcoholics into therapy. Society has stopped waiting for the alcoholic to go for help. To the delight of some health workers and the dismay of certain civil rights advocates, each day legally competent alcoholics, who often live with families, face no physical danger, and are indistinguishable from their neighbors, are being compelled to take treatment they would not accept voluntarily.

Many states, for example, require alcoholics on public assistance — 15 percent of all recipients — to seek treatment. In New York City in 1981, nearly 9,000 alcoholics on welfare were threatened with a loss of benefits unless they agreed to become hospital patients. Ten percent refused and lost their support. Recipients unable to get or keep a job because of drinking were labeled as alcoholic. Averaging about fifteen outpatient visits over a six-month period, these alcoholics received intensive group and individual therapy aimed at making them recognize they can cope with life without alcohol's euphoria.

Most states require arrested drunk drivers to be interviewed by social workers who determine whether the driver simply had one too many or is an alcoholic, a person with a history of drinking problems. About 25 percent of the offenders are alcoholic, and they are required to get hospital treatment or their fines will be increased and their licenses suspended for long terms. In New York State, 5,150 alcoholics convicted of drunk driving in 1981 were pressured into accepting treatment. These were not skid-row types: 75 percent were working regularly, in contrast to the 25 percent of all regular alcoholism clinic patients who had steady jobs. In California, the "1982 landmark drunk driving law which mandated (the choice of) harsher penalties or treatment according to all indications will dramatically further increase the flow of clients to treatment agencies," concluded a report by the University of California at Berkeley's Alcohol Research Group.

Oregon goes further, telling the arrested alcoholic to choose jail or probation, with the condition of treatment that includes "at least the supplying of disulfiram or any other agent that interferes with normal metabolic degradation of alcohol in the body" (see Appendix A). Sold under the name of Antabuse, the drug disulfiram makes a person violently ill — throbbing head, copious vomiting, chest pains, hypertension — if he or she tries to drink within three days after taking it. Antabuse forces the alcoholic to remain sober during treatment and thus effectively participate in alcoholism therapy. Only a small percentage of alcoholic patients agree to take the drug voluntarily.

"Mandating Antabuse, which is a powerful chemical, increases the anger of these arrested drivers and increases resistance to treatment," says Barbara Grider, head of the Alcohol Safety Action Program in Poland. While 400 of her 500 patients used to be on court-ordered Antabuse, the number has dropped to about 50 because she has convinced most judges not to require it in the treatment choice offered the arrested alcoholic. She adds, however, if "one of our coerced patients isn't cooperating we'll go back to probation and get Antabuse written in as a requirement."

If a Delaware family court decides an alcoholic's behavior is "imperiling a family relationship" (for example, because of drinking a husband is not working and providing support or acts threateningly toward his family), the judge can order the person into treatment (see Appendix A). Refusal to go is contempt of court, which means a fine or jail. Under this threat, about 500 alcoholics have chosen treatment since 1971.

Similarly, in 1982, New Jersey Governor Tom Kean signed a new family court act. The law states that when the court has a "juvenile-family crisis" — a youth running away from home, failing to attend school regularly, or committing a crime — and when a parent's alcoholism contributed to the youngster's behavior, the judge can order the father or mother to accept treatment (see Appendix A). If he or she refuses this therapy, the parent faces contempt of court and a fine or jail sentence.

These powerful either-or threats offer no real choice, critics argue, and so violate the Constitution's rights of privacy and protection against cruel and inhuman punishment. Opponents also fear that these laws may have a widespread effect and lead to public acceptance of other measures that pressure into treatment people whose behaviors conflict with society's norms.

Yet no state law has been declared unconstitutional. Dr. Ronald Catanzaro, director of the Palm Beach Institute, a major treatment facility, favors coercive laws. "All alcoholics are forced in some way into treatment — threats from a spouse, child, doctor, employer. Laws are no different, except they can affect far more alcoholics."

No national statistics exist. In New York State last year, approximately 15,000 alcoholics, arrested for drunk driving or on welfare, were coerced into treatment. Extrapolating from this statistic gives a national figure of 235,000 legally competent alcoholics being compelled to get treatment each year. This national estimate of nearly a quarter of a million people may be too low, since New York State has no coercion procedure for alcoholics in family court, and in New York

City, where nearly half the population lives, the police admit they avoid pursuing drunk drivers in order to concentrate on street crime.

"Legal coercion has become a widely accepted and permanent element in the treatment of the person with alcohol-related problems," concludes a review of these laws in the *Journal of Drug Issues*. "Although legal coercion originates with and is controlled by the legal system, alcohol treatment programs have come to rely heavily on it to identify alcoholics, to bring alcoholics into treatment, and to help them in treatment."

This approach to curbing alcoholism reflects an international trend. The findings of a sixty-nation survey by the International Council on Alcohol and Addictions provide many examples of foreign governments legally pressuring alcoholics into treatment:

● Government-ordered treatment in Poland results in 44,000 outpatient visits yearly, which accounts for 38 percent of all alcoholics who receive outpatient help. It forces 6,400 Poles, or 40 percent of alcoholic inpatients, into residential facilities for up to two years.

● In Finland, mandated treatment increased from 10,658 in 1968 to 14,344 in 1978, "despite the fact that even the voluntary care of alcoholics — alcoholism clinics, Alcoholics Anonymous — had expanded enormously in the same time," notes Martti Voipio, former secretary general of the League of Finnish Temperance Organizations.

● In Czechoslovakia about 6,000 persons each year are pressured by legal threats to go for treatment.

● Of the 1,678 Dutch men treated in 1978 for alcoholism, about 20 percent were coerced into this therapy by a court or government order.

● Forced measures now account for 4 percent of the Norwegian alcoholics going for counseling.

● Arab nations, which because of severe religious and legal restrictions have enjoyed the lowest rate of alcoholism, are also attracted to this movement. Normally, severe punishment is their means of preventing alcoholism: public drunkenness in Egypt, for example, can result in six months in prison. However, a 1976 meeting in Iraq concluded, "Arab countries are invited to include in their penal laws articles concerning compulsory measures to be executed by courts for sending alcohol addicts to psychosocial treatment."

The appeal of these laws is enhanced by the international publicity about alcoholism's spreading damage. Alcohol abuse now consumes 30 percent of Chile's health budget and results in 25 to 45 percent of all general medical admissions in France (public hospitals treating the indigent report higher percentages).

In 1975, Bror Rexed, head of health services in Sweden, called alcoholism that country's greatest social problem. He noted that alcohol abuse among criminals was five times greater than in the noncriminal population and caused one-third of the admissions to psychiatric care.

Despite the Koran's prohibition against drinking, the United Arab Emirates "may be the only Arab country to have its own chapter of Alcoholics Anonymous," comments the writer Eric Ambler. Even in food-poor and Moslem Somali, Colonel Osman Ahmed Hussein, of the Somali Police Force, says, "The biggest percentage of our population are traditional nomads, who live in rural areas where liquors and drugs are not heard of. But how long this will continue is questionable."

The World Health Organization has called for help for the third world. "The evidence of increasing damage in a large number of developing countries suggests alcohol-related problems constitute an important obstacle to their socio-economic development and are likely to overwhelm their health resources unless appropriate measures are taken."

Wealth is no protection. Although getting rich on offshore oil, the province of Newfoundland has found that between 1970 and 1980 teenage drinking increased by 90 percent, and alcohol liver cirrhosis by 40 percent. In the fast-growing areas of Norway near the North Sea oil operations, alcohol-related criminal offenses now exceed all other criminal problems.

In Portugal, which along with its Mediterranean neighbors

has enjoyed a history of relatively low alcohol abuse, the director of Oporto's Medical-Legal Institute, J. Pinto Da Costa says, "This subject of the law and alcoholism can be ignored no longer, even if it will shake certain preconceptions. We must oblige them (alcoholics) to pay for the damages they commit and one way of doing this is to treat them compulsorily."

Similarly in Italy, Dr. Daniele Striani, ex-magistrate of the Supreme Court in Rome, notes, "The number of alcoholics is increasing, even among the young people, often related to or as an alternative to (other) drug addiction." Italy established a commission in 1977 to study the adoption of coercive treatment legislation, but it failed to reach a consensus on what to do.

Judge Stephen North, of Nashville, discussed the need for new legal alternatives in sentencing alcoholics in the United States at a 1978 Trial Judges Conference on Creative Alternatives to Prison: "I think the Los Angeles Police Department did a study on all arrests. Alcohol was involved in the neighborhood of 68 percent of all burglaries. Almost all family disputes involved problems with alcohol. Virtually all child abuse and wife abuse cases involved alcohol. A large number of murders and robberies involved alcohol. In fact, they indicated that in spite of the glamour of the hard drugs, alcohol was probably a more substantial factor in crime than heroin or the other hard drugs that have gotten more of the publicity and perhaps more of the money and interest. It seems to me that if we could provide treatment alternatives to people with alcohol problems and thereby allow them to solve their problems, that we are accomplishing a great deal more, both from the standpoint of the safety of the community and from the standpoint of the benefit of the individual, than the more traditional methods of sentencing."

The Illness Impact

Punishment was originally believed to be the way to stop an

alcoholic's drinking. In 1606, England declared public intoxication a crime with "An Act For Repressing The Odious And Loathsome Sin of Drunkenness." The United States adopted this view and found that the public drunk was the most frequent resident of its jails. Usually lacking a job, education, good health, and a family, the inebriate was the toughest person for prison social workers to counsel. Chronic drunks passed into and out of jails, with society paying the high cost and prison officials complaining they could not break the alcoholism cycle.

DeWitt Easter's obituary in the December 5, 1967, *Washington Post* describes the change in approach to alcoholism:

> DeWitt Easter, the 62-year-old skid-row drunk whose name is attached to a landmark court case that changed the way alcoholics are treated in Washington, died yesterday in D.C. General Hospital.
>
> He died of massive complications that followed second- and third-degree burns he suffered in a bed fire November 11 while a patient at George Washington University Hospital. He was later transferred to D.C. General.
>
> Mr. Easter, who had been arrested more than 70 times since he became an alcoholic 30 years ago, had been a patient in the city's hospitals and rehabilitation facilities almost constantly since the U.S. Court of Appeals for the District ruled in his case on March 31, 1966, that alcoholism must be treated as an illness, not a crime.
>
> A frail plasterer with steady, steel-blue eyes, Mr. Easter recognized the importance of the court's ruling. But he could not stop drinking. His latest hospitalization came after a two-month drinking spree.

The Easter case was part of a legal trend in the 1960s and 1970s. Drawing on worldwide medical opinion that alcoholism was an illness needing treatment, states declared they would no longer jail the public intoxicant since he was sick, although disorderly conduct and other drunken offenses could be punished. Today public drunkenness has been decriminalized by thirty-one states.

Recognizing alcoholism as a medical illness, states instead began passing laws to pressure into treatment the great majority of alcoholics. These people are more stable than the public inebriate, more treatable, and responsible for the greatest part of alcohol abuse's costs (only about 5 percent of all alcoholics live on skid rows). In the late 1970s, for example, New York State repealed both its criminal law against public drunkenness and the procedure of involuntary civil commitment to a state institution for a mentally ill alcoholic likely to harm himself. The state meanwhile passed legislation that required alcoholics arrested for drunk driving and those receiving welfare benefits to seek treatment.

These new coercion laws give the alcoholic a choice of accepting treatment or receiving stiff penalties. The old involuntary commitment regulations, which many states still have, target the alcoholic who is deranged or unable to care for himself. Doctors, courts, and hospitals try to avoid this procedure. Doctors who sign an affidavit on a person's mental state may face a court challenge from the individual's relatives. Facilities do not want patients who are committed against their will and who may refuse or be unable to cooperate in therapy. In addition, treatment institutions must make time-consuming reappearances in court to prove that an involuntary patient should participate in periods of long, necessary therapy.

The process of involuntary commitment, however, affects only impaired alcoholics. A 1967 federal review of alcoholism laws indicated the growing sentiment to change these laws' reach: "The idea that some risk to society, or slight judgmental impairment, are insufficient to authorize compulsory treatment may be disturbing to treatment-minded persons, because often treatment may be more successful before the condition reaches the stage where any of the proper bases for commitment may be involved."

The recognition of alcoholism as a medical illness also led to the creation of "employee assistance programs" in the nation's large corporations during the 1960s and 1970s. As an ill employee, the alcoholic was entitled to a company's sick-leave and health insurance benefits. However, the alcoholic usually would not admit he had a problem, and meanwhile his poor work was hurting the firm. In response, increasing numbers of corporations adopted programs to confront the alcoholic worker: "Go for help and your job will be waiting for you. If you refuse or fail to complete treatment, then we'll judge you on your performance. That could mean a demotion or being fired."

Corporations reported that between 60 and 80 percent of these employees completed treatment and returned to their jobs. Industrial programs attracted a lot of publicity and influenced legislators. If corporations could successfully practice early intervention, why not government's far more pervasive legal system?

Critics questioned how well coercion supervised by impersonal government and court workers would work, in contrast to an employer's empathy for a longtime alcoholic employee. Supporters argued that if the success rate of government efforts was even half of that experienced by corporations, the nation's number of alcoholics would fall dramatically, since government would affect far greater numbers of alcoholics.

In the multinational survey by the International Council on Alcohol and Addictions, government agencies stated they were adopting coercive measures because they refused to do nothing while alcohol abuse's publicized toll grew, even if definitive proof was not yet available on the percentage of alcoholics who would recover from legal intervention. Although Alcoholics Anonymous has no exact proof on the success of legal threats, its literature states it will cooperate with coercive procedures — for example, informing a court whether an alcoholic is attending meetings — since "any kind of message carrying [on the need for treatment] is a success for us."

Dr. Jaroslav Skála, director of Prague's Alcoholism Clinic, says in Czechoslovakia, "the efficiency of the treatment for involuntary patients is roughly two or three times less successful than for voluntary patients. But compulsory treatment is better than no treatment."

"I'd guess about 75 percent of the alcoholics forced into treatment through our law recover and stay abstinent. But, no, we've never studied this," admits William Davies, director of family court operations in Delaware. Similarly, city and state officials concerned with New York's coercive treatment programs staunchly support these efforts, though they admit they have not evaluated either the laws' effectiveness or costs to the public.

There have been a few studies of the effects of these new laws: A 1981 review of alcoholics arrested for drunk driving and ordered to get treatment at a New York City municipal hospital found that 57 percent of them began drinking after just two months in treatment. "That's about the same high failure rate as our voluntary patients experience," says Dr. Enoch Gordis, the director of Elmhurst Hospital. "We can claim that the threats of legal coercion don't make our alcoholic patients especially motivated to accept treatment. Or we can say that at least a number of people do become aware of their need for treatment because of court pressure and obviously some will stay sober."

German facilities show "that those treated on a compulsory basis fare no worse than those who are there voluntarily," says Dr. Herbert Ziegler, director of an addiction therapy facility in Hamm. "Evidence frequently indicates that one-third of patients are successfully treated, one-third show improvement in their general condition, and one-third show no improvement."

Most coerced alcoholics receive outpatient treatment—once a week counseling sessions for about six months—rather than the more costly and intensive residential therapy, which usually lasts a month. Residential treatment, however, can dramatically increase the success rate for court-ordered as well as voluntary patients, according to Minnesota's well-known Hazelden rehabilitation center.

The clinic evaluated the 288 alcoholics who had been coerced into its facility in 1974–75 by courts for "a variety of legal problems such as driving offenses, family disturbances, and juvenile offenses." During their thirty-day stay these patients received lectures, readings, individual counseling, and group therapy aimed at overcoming the alcoholic's sense of hopelessness, the belief that he or she must drink to cope with life. The treatment results were compared to the experiences of 2,662 voluntary patients seen during this time. "Of those referred by the court, 79.2 percent completed treatment in contrast to 74 percent of the noncommitted patients." One year later 49.4 percent of the voluntary and 50.7 percent of the mandated patients were still sober. Hazelden concluded its survey enthusiastically: "Does judicial commitment . . . work? Based on the patient follow-up data reported here, the answer is 'yes.'"

Dr. A. J. Auret, director general of South Africa's Department of Health, Welfare and Pensions, claims that country's success rate with court-mandated patients, who receive five to seven months of therapy at a residential clinic, is 60 percent. The criterion used in determining the success rate is "that the alcoholic has been successfully integrated into the community and his family for a minimum period of twelve months."

Such findings may lead to development of a new, middle-range of alcoholism services: a treatment regimen that is more intensive than the once-a-week outpatient therapy but of less duration and cost than the traditional one-month residential stay. Such a program, called the Evening and Weekend Alcoholism Treatment Project, is being tested in Washington, D.C., for employees of the Department of Health and Human Services.

As compulsory treatment spreads, hospital staffs will increase their ability to work with these patients and so also their success rate, argues Dr. Marlene Paley, of the Long Island Center for Problem Drinking. Reviewing the literature in a study, *Problems Presented By Alcoholic Clients,* Michael Jacobs found many alcohol therapists view court-mandated "individuals as poor risks for treatment. They are required to be sober for their counseling sessions, but more often than not that is their only obligation." Dr. Paley, however, says her experiences with drunk drivers forced into treatment indicates that "when the staff can demonstrate to clients that they are fortunate in undergoing treatment and that the treatment is not intended as punishment, the results are positive."

Treatment's Techniques and Scope

Commenting on the welfare recipient who is compelled to accept treatment at her facility, Ellen Morehouse, a psychiatric social worker with the Westchester (New York) Community Mental Health Services, says: "Often in the beginning interview, a mandated alcoholic will deny the extent of his drinking and will explain that he is attending merely to satisfy his worker and thus ensure maintenance of his assistance grant. It cannot be assumed, however, that this client is unmotivated. It is possible that he would like to stop drinking and has tried but has been so uncomfortable with withdrawal symptoms or psychiatric symptoms that he feels he has no other choice but to continue drinking."

Hearing a discussion of the new coercive treatment laws at a recent meeting of the board of directors of a large alcoholism agency, a woman suddenly rose, obviously upset, eyes wet with tears, and called out that her son was now in treatment. She had convinced him to go. "What he needs is love, love! Not laws."

She is at least partly correct: studies show that the chance of successfully helping any alcoholic relates directly to the sympathy and support expressed by the therapist. A "positive treatment relationship" can be created with coerced alcoholics, Morehouse emphasizes, if therapists demonstrate that the patients are their main concern.

Morehouse advises, for example, that if the mandated alcoholic arrives drunk — which frequently happens — the worker should not invoke a hospital rule of automatically refusing to see him. "The therapist may need to have the intoxicated alcoholic pass several hours in the waiting area so that he can sober up before starting the intake interview, as opposed to sending him away and telling him he has to come alcohol-free tomorrow."

If the alcoholic drops out of treatment prematurely, "the mandating government agency must be notified," agrees Morehouse. "Before notification, however, every effort should be made to reinvolve the alcoholic in treatment. For example, the therapist might make a home visit or send a letter advising the alcoholic of the steps that will be taken if he is not heard from within a given period of time."

Gateway Community Services, an alcoholism treatment program in Jacksonville, Florida, boasts that 25 percent of its patients are there under court order, the highest percentage of any Florida facility, and are successfully treated because the staff has special empathy. Michael Hanrahan, an administrative law judge with the Coast Guard and one of the program's founders, says: "A few years back the city of Jacksonville's alcohol rehabilitation program left a lot to be desired. Most of the staff were low-level civil servants who had little empathy for the alcoholic and understanding of alcoholism. It was then that a group of business executives, all members of AA, banded together and formed Gateway."

This sympathy also has to be firm — "tough love," alcoholism counselors call it. Gayle Rosellini, who supervised a drunk driving program for seven years, comments that, "Tough means actively confronting the alcoholic denial system, demanding client *participation* rather than attendance, and demanding abstinence documented by monitored Antabuse and mandatory, regular, and random breath tests (to determine if a patient is drinking). It also means throwing out the ridiculous notion that a drinking alcoholic will freely and honestly admit his true drinking behavior. Alcoholic drivers won't quit drinking and won't quit driving drunk unless we *make* them."

"The efficiency of such forms of coercive treatment is

gradually improving although it is not yet satisfactory," comments Dr. Skála of Prague's Alcoholism Clinic. Czech treatment professionals, for example, arrange group sessions with a ratio of two voluntary clients to every coerced patient, feeling this is the best way to get mandated alcoholics to participate in counseling.

"Nonrigid staffs are needed," notes Alice Petropoulos, director of the counseling department of the New York City Affiliate of the National Council on Alcoholism. A psychologist, Petropoulos and her staff see New York's coerced patients at their angriest stage, just after they have been told by the welfare department or traffic court that they need alcoholism treatment. "These patients will vary dramatically, both in personal and drinking backgrounds," says Petropoulos, offering as examples four patients:

Arrested for drunk driving, Dan was in his twenties, married, and a construction worker. His mother was an active alcoholic. Dan began drinking as a teenager and now always "drank to get drunk."

When first seen in counseling, Dan was already experiencing two basic alcoholism signs: blackouts, which mean a loss of memory, and high tolerance or the need for ever more alcohol to get high. He said he drank because his marriage was unhappy and denied he was alcoholic.

After attending ten outpatient sessions, once a week, of group therapy, Dan admitted he had rationalized his drinking behavior and needed help to stay abstinent. He agreed to join AA. Eight months later, Dan was still attending AA meetings but drinking sporadically. Previously, however, he had been a daily drinker, and now he was considering entering a hospital for Antabuse therapy.

Roger also was arrested for drunk driving and coerced into therapy. A forty-year-old, unskilled worker, he had been a daily drinker for almost nine years. He was married and had two young children. Roger's drinking had begun to disrupt his job and family life. He was very quiet and acquiescent when starting treatment at a comprehensive city outpatient program.

Two months later, Roger dropped out of this program and was drinking again. Since he knew the state would eventually reinstate his license, whether or not he finished treatment, Roger had no reason to stay sober. Unlike Dan, the outpatient sessions he attended were not enough to motivate him to change.

Martin, forty-two, divorced, was on welfare and referred by the Department of Social Services. He was irritated at having to see a counselor in order to keep his public assistance. Having six or more drinks a day, Martin had a twenty-year history of alcohol abuse.

Contacted three months later, Martin said he was attending counseling sessions twice a week at an outpatient program. The clinic verified this and said he was responding well. Apparently the threat of the loss of his public support was sufficient to make him complete treatment.

A fifty-year-old professional musician, Ivan was a Russian immigrant who had been arrested for drunk driving. He immediately became a member of AA, even before the court suspended his license. This driving arrest as well as a family argument over it interrupted his ten-year drinking habit.

In contrast to many arrested drivers coerced into taking treatment, Ivan was very cooperative and insightful. He planned to continue in AA and periodically take Antabuse at times of stress.

Six weeks later, Ivan was still sober and attending AA regularly. His counselor believed this case was atypical because of the client's high self-motivation.

Evaluating treatment results is difficult. An alcoholic completes therapy or drops out prematurely. He starts drinking again or stays sober or at least experiences fewer alcohol-caused problems. How much can be attributed to (or blamed on) the skills and attitude of the particular therapist? How much comes out of the extra services provided by a specific facility, for example, physical exercise, job counseling, the requirements or lack of them that a patient participate in custodial work, and so on? If a coerced alcoholic recovers, can it be argued that he had reached a time in his life when he would have gone for help voluntarily? If a patient drops out of counseling, was he at a stage in his drinking when no treatment could have succeeded?

"It's not likely we'll ever have a consensus in the field of what is the right treatment," concludes an article in the journal *Alcoholism: Clinical and Experimental Research.* Evaluating the effects of an antibiotic is far different than knowing whether a drinker's behavior and attitudes have been permanently changed by treatment, and if so, why.

It is a sense of what should work, rather than scientific proof, that has long dictated alcoholism treatment's growth. This therapy "owes its existence more to historical processes than to science," commented the *Lancet,* the British medical journal. "It is possible to discern the deposits, akin to geological layers, of a sequence of therapeutic fashions — the residue of almost forgotten enthusiasm for inpatient psychotherapy units, for group processes and the therapeutic community, for family therapy, and later for community psychiatry." Coercion into treatment is the next phase in this "historical process."

If coercion laws forced an additional 10 percent of alcoholics to seek treatment, then 1 million more alcoholics would be exposed to therapy. Treated as outpatients for fifteen visits over a six-month period — the New York City average for coerced patients — their charge to the nation would roughly be $900 million, since Medicaid pays about $60 for each outpatient visit.

Washington estimates that alcoholism costs the nation $50 billion a year. If 30 percent (the average success rate) of these 1 million coerced alcoholics became permanently sober or at least able to work regularly, the nation's damage from alcoholism would be reduced by 3 percent or $1.5 billion and more than pay for the treatment costs. The potential payoffs in both financial and human terms will maintain pressure to expand the scope of compulsory procedures. This scope can become very broad.

In America, as in most nations, for example, about 50 percent of all voluntary alcoholic patients drop out of treatment within thirty days. Czechoslovakia has a law that addresses the problem of alcoholics who refuse to go to treatment or leave prematurely after an employer has told them to get help: "Those patients who manifest a negative attitude to treatment are assigned to type C (compulsory) treatment. The period of commitment to the institution is at least six months" (see Appendix A).

Would the threat of a lengthy stay at an inpatient facility decrease the number of alcoholics who voluntarily admit the need for help? Or is it the way to solve the problem of so many alcoholics leaving treatment "against medical advice"? Would the Supreme Court uphold as constitutional laws that in effect recognize worker productivity as a right the state can protect?

A law has been passed by the legislature of Prince Edward Island, but not yet signed by the province's premier, that would give the police the right to determine if someone is alcoholic and to take the person from his house and to a treatment facility for seventy-two hours. No court order is necessary (see Appendix A).

Dr. Mark Triantafillou, the addiction services director in Charlottetown, Prince Edward Island, argues for this procedure: "Normally, nothing can be done until a domestic fight results in someone actually being hurt or in danger — then the police can knock on the door to break it up, or take someone to jail. Or an abused spouse can go to court and obtain an order of protection, return home, get beaten up by the drunk husband — and then have the right to call the police. Our idea is instead to get in there early. Get alcoholics to help rather than jail, and while the family is still together." Triantafillou adds that his island has a small population, which he believes prevents police from using the law to harass citizens. He readily recognizes the fear in impersonal big cities of allowing police to enter homes to take someone off to a clinic and suggests the procedure not be used there.

"Anything which gives the authority such sweeping powers has to be viewed with alarm and repugnance," says Alan Borovoy of the Canadian Civil Liberties Association, "whether in a rural province or city. The law is bad anywhere, and I hope the premier will never sign it."

If allowing the police to enter an alcoholic's home puts fear into many, what about the possibility of forced injections for someone identified as an alcoholic? The technique for implanting Antabuse was developed in the 1950s in France and has recently been refined and used increasingly in Eastern Europe as well as France. Implants eliminate a present problem of clinic staffs: alcoholics sometimes pretend to swallow their disulfiram, hiding the pill in their mouths or concealing it elsewhere.

Oral disulfiram lasts for three days. With implanted pellets the chemical remains in the alcoholic's body for about six months. As the drug makes its taker violently ill if he or she drinks, the implanted patient gains a lengthy period of sobriety and can better participate in counseling sessions. A 1981 review of the scientific literature by Dr. Marc Schukit of the Veterans Administration Center in San Diego concluded that studies increasingly show implants improve the chance of treatment success. The only side effects are severe inflammation and abscesses.

Although coercively administering oral Antabuse is already sanctioned by one state, Schukit worries about jumping to the next step, "There is not enough data to justify forcing patients to take the medication (through implants) when they do not want to do so." The present lack of data stems from the difficulty of knowing exactly how long implanted disulfiram is effective. This obstacle may soon disappear.

Dr. Michael Phillips of Georgetown University has developed

a small sweat patch that when taped to a patient's skin indicates whether a person has been drinking during the past ten days. Phillips says, "I can foresee a future where those alcoholics physically able (they have no heart, liver, or emotional problems) will come to a doctor's office say every four months for a disulfiram implant, and meanwhile they'll be in therapy."

Dr. Yedy Israel of the University of Toronto predicts, "Disulfiram is being used with some success in alcoholics. The major problem in this therapy relates to drug compliance. Considering the advanced state of art in these areas, an active search for a highly effective form of disulfiram could be fruitful in about a decade. Such a substance which could be implanted . . ."

The Swedish Board of Health and Welfare has announced it will devote more attention to studying disulfiram implants. Officials point especially to a study in neighboring Norway that showed 25 percent of the implant patients were sober three and a half years after treatment and 45 percent of the others had improved their lives through reduced drinking or extended periods of abstinence.

A study of 5,578 alcoholism patients found that the two most important indicators of success were taking Antabuse in the hospital and attending Alcoholics Anonymous meetings regularly after release. "Nevertheless, we still do not know whether Antabuse keeps patients sober or whether willingness to take it identifies (motivated) patients who would do as well without it," the survey concluded.

Reports also indicate, not surprisingly, that the more severe the legal threat the less chance that the court-ordered alcoholic will drop out of treatment prematurely. Reviewing the studies on compulsory outpatient treatment for municipal court offenders (usually chronic alcoholics arrested for disorderly acts), Dr. Chad Emrick, a psychologist with the Veterans Administration Medical Center in Denver, concluded that this treatment was "not more effective than voluntary outpatient therapy or no treatment," because these alcoholics usually disappeared from the counseling programs. "But for state prison parolees who faced a severe penalty for not complying with treatment, compulsory outpatient treatment was shown to be more effective than voluntary outpatient therapy."

Since the more severe coercive techniques tend to produce better treatment results the expansion of these procedures should be monitored to make sure the rights of the individual alcoholic are not forgotten (see Chapter 7). For example, Jacek Morawski of Warsaw's Psychoneurological Institute says that Poland has given compulsory treatment laws too much power and reach in the name of successful therapy, and this has created problems. A study of one treatment group revealed that one-third of the patients did not belong there. Yet, Morawski admits, without the country's strong laws "many alcoholics would never have experienced treatment."

Because mandatory treatment regulations charge that a person's disruptive behavior at home, inability to support a family, or chaotic driving are caused by alcoholism, they force a court or government agency to inspect and evaluate an individual's private behavior. In Germany this results in special discomfort, notes Dr. Herbert Ziegler, director of the addictions program in Hamm: "Negative experiences emanating from the period between 1933 and 1945 continue to play a major role in discussion of this question." Still Germany has authorized coercive treatment laws aimed at teenage alcoholics.

South Africa's success rate with court-mandated patients is 60 percent, far exceeding the U.S.'s 30 percent average for all alcoholics in therapy. These South African alcoholics most often stay at a residential center and can be required to visit a social worker regularly for a follow-up period of up to three years. A failure to report during this period violates the probation order and results in the alcoholic's being ordered back for more therapy. In addition, the family in South Africa is asked to become involved in the treatment. U.S. legal procedures do not invoke such a long follow-up requirement or family involvement, yet good follow-up and family participation improve treatment success rates.

Even if copying the more intensive South African treatment procedure is desired, financing it presents a major obstacle. South Africa's monthly cost of residential therapy is $600 per person, while the cost in America is more than $3,000, and clinics charging $8,000 and $10,000 are not uncommon. Austria, whose cost of living equals if not exceeds that of the United States, has a one-month charge of about $1,870, roughly 35 percent less than the U.S. average.

The high cost of U.S. health is one of the impediments to the growth of coercive government treatment. "Ramon Lopez knew his father, but he also knew that he was perpetually unemployed and often drunk," noted a recent *New Yorker* article that described the typical problems of the poor in the big cities.

If New York City's family court adopted the Delaware law of forcing parents with drinking problems into treatment, "our clinics would be overloaded immediately," a city health official admits. "We are reluctant about favoring the quick adoption of these compulsory laws, since we'd have to come up with new treatment resources immediately. These costs would be staggering. The savings in people and money could be fantastic — but they come later. And the savings accrue to society generally and will not necessarily be passed through to our system."

A 1982 study of nine private and public alcoholism facilities in Minnesota and Wisconsin found that the number of their patients still on welfare six months after treatment fell by 50 percent and was cut in half again one year after discharge. The author, Norman Hoffman, said, in addition, "we found a 40 percent drop in medical and psychiatric-related problems, a 35 percent drop in outpatient visits to the doctor, and an 85 percent drop in arrests."

Government's overwhelming concern about immediate costs led New York State to approve in 1981 an order of protection law to prevent domestic violence. This law allows the family court judge to require the parent who is threatening his family "to participate in an educational program," but the court specifically cannot mandate any treatment because of the financial fear: "Such an order (of protection) may require such person to participate in an educational program and to pay the costs thereof if the person has the means to do so, provided however that nothing contained herein shall be deemed to require payment of the costs of any such program by the state or any political subdivision thereof."

Martin Adelman smiles when he is told that civil rights advocates can rely on the stiff costs of health and social services and the lack of new funding for treatment programs as a restraint on compulsory treatment measures. An attorney involved in alcoholism issues who successfully sued New York City's police department for failure to hire recovered alcoholics, Adelman believes that the new legal pressures on alcoholics can set dangerous precedents for society generally. He predicts: "Many of these coercive laws eventually will be challenged and defeated in court. Courts are where the real restraint is."

Adelman believes that if an alcoholic commits a crime the court should give him a choice of punishment or treatment. "That makes sense. Society has been legally harmed. But not this coercion through welfare and family court, where there is no legal violation.

"The welfare and family court procedures also single out the alcoholic for not contributing sufficiently to his family or society. But so are a lot of other sick, disoriented, and lazy people failing to provide this support. When the law picks on just one group of people — well, you've set a dangerous example.

"Drinking is a private behavior. This country has long protected the sanctity of private behaviors, especially those done in the home. These coercion laws can lead one day to a social worker charging not that the person is an alcoholic, but just that if he drank less he'd then work harder, contribute more support, pay more attention to the kids. And that's probably true. But then there'd be a legal standard for how much you can drink, or how much you have to earn if you do drink.

"Sure, some of these laws can create a breakthrough in alcoholism. But it will be the courts that must eventually be relied on to determine their scope. Not treatment costs or other outside factors."

Discussing the Prince Edward Island law, Adelman emphasizes that the Constitution's Fourth Amendment — "the right of people to be secure in their persons, houses" — would strike down any attempt in the United States to allow police to take an alcoholic to a treatment facility just because he or she acted inappropriately at home. But Adelman was asked how the Supreme Court might rule given these facts: Families recognize the alcoholic among them far sooner than employers, traffic cops, criminal courts, or any other outside group. Treatment statistics prove that the earlier the alcoholic enters a facility the greater the chance he will do well, since his physical and emotional needs for alcohol and the social and health damage from drinking will be at their lowest points. Families suffer from alcohol abuse, but only a minority are able to coax their drinkers into voluntary treatment. Frustrated spouses constantly tell alcoholism counselors they wished a law existed that would have compelled treatment for the alcoholic as soon as the problem was apparent. Isn't it reasonable, therefore, to allow a family to petition a court to order treatment for a parent or child who is obviously alcoholic but whose illness hasn't progressed to the point where he has threatened or harmed someone, stopped providing financial support, or placed a child "in crisis"?

"No," Adelman replied. "Drinking, even as an addicted alcoholic, is still a private behavior that the Constitution should protect until a person actually violates the law." Adelman admitted, however, that if research could ever prove that very early legal intervention in families would "nearly always" result in successful treatment, courts might approve this more encompassing procedure. The Fourth Amendment protects only against "unreasonable searches and seizures," Adelman reasoned. "Public opinion shapes the law and is influenced by practical arguments about what is reasonable. If the alcoholic parent will almost surely become sober, then this early coercion could be allowed."

Future Changes and Arguments

Most of those opposed to legally pressuring treatment on alcoholics rely heavily on the present scarcity of studies concerning which alcoholics will benefit from these procedures. An opponent of the laws mandating oral disulfiram (Antabuse) for alcoholics, Dr. Corey Marco, a medical doctor and attorney, hedges his civil liberties arguments by writing, "Furthermore, the drug appears to be only marginally effective in helping those . . . who lack the motivation to cooperate with treatment."

The American Civil Liberties Union of Oregon has complained about making Antabuse ingestion a condition of probation, declaring that court probation workers have failed to check adequately medical backgrounds to identify persons who may become physically or emotionally ill from the drug. As a result, some alcoholic offenders have become sick. This could be considered "cruel and inhuman punishment" and thus an unconstitutional procedure. Still the ACLU did not absolutely oppose this law but instead told "Oregon's trial judges to restudy the question of whether . . . tighter and better medical approval and supervision procedures should be required."

Paddy Bruce, a member of the Prince Edward Island Advisory Committee on Alcohol and Drug Addiction Prevention Services, dissented to the passage of the province's compulsory treatment law. She declared: "The incredible paradox of not locking people up in jails for being drunk but instead locking them up in treatment centers — they are still locked up. The ethical concern is with making persons with alcoholism or other addiction problems into second-class citizens by taking away their basic civil and human rights. Government has pledged itself to reduce the numbers of laws and regulations which affect the lives of ordinary citizens on P.E.I. The recommendations of my colleagues with regard to compulsory detainment go against this direction and would almost certainly raise objections from civil liberties and human rights groups." But, Bruce concluded, "As ethically abhorrent as locking people up 'for their own good' is to me, I would seriously consider it as an alternative if it had been shown to offer results."

This practical argument should weaken as facilities gain experience with mandated patients and as more clinics produce success rates that equal those of voluntary patients. As Dr. Jaroslav Skála said about Czechoslovakia, "the efficiency of such forms of treatment is gradually improving, although it is not yet satisfactory."

Drunk drivers forced to take treatment in Phoenix were studied by a research team led by Paul Swenson. It followed 351 men for eighteen months and found that at the end of this period none of the men were abstinent or drinking significantly less. The researchers questioned the program's procedures: the delays before the men entered treatment, the manner in which people were handled after arrest, and whether changing the length of treatment could have made a difference. Swenson wrote, "Although the present study failed to detect positive effects of court-mandated DWI [Driving While Intoxicated] treatment programs in Phoenix, the future of such programs seems assured, especially those that support themselves through client fees and function as part of an efficiently operating judicial system. Of course, this does not mean that existing research strategies and treatment plans cannot be changed to increase the likelihood that such programs will achieve their stated objectives."

Since coercion laws are increasing more quickly than the knowledge of their effectiveness, public disputes can be expected. The history of British Columbia's 1979 call for compulsory treatment of heroin addicts, one of the most argued-about forced treatment efforts in North America, provides a glimpse at the kind of controversy that might arise.

Through this program identified narcotic users could be required to take treatment. Designed to reach 2,500 addicts, the program's expected cost was $13 million a year, ten times the amount the province was then spending on heroin addiction. The health minister, Robert McClelland, defended this expense in terms of the need for a "a new, fresh attack" on heroin addiction.

To avoid the delays of a court review, police would take an addict to a panel of health professionals, which could order the individual to a special treatment center for a six-month period. The term was renewable for up to three years. There was no right to counsel or a court review until the addict actually entered the facility.

Civil rights groups immediately challenged the law, since it lacked the traditional legal protections and affected a person who had violated no law but simply was "judged dependent on a narcotic." McClelland defended this procedure as necessary for helping the heroin addict who resisted treatment. "What we're going to have is the most humane and probably the most comprehensive program ever tried in North America. This is not a concentration camp we're setting up. We're not reverting to Nazi Germany." As time approached to start the program, the legal attacks grew and addicts dropped out of the province's voluntary treatment programs, fearful of being sent to the new long-term facility.

The *Journal,* of Toronto, Canada, one of the leading newspapers covering alcohol and drugs, reported that the new facility "looks like a holiday camp — the indoor swimming pool, the gym, the green down to the lakeshore." While reporters described the institution, opponents passed out leaflets that compared this press tour to a well-known Red Cross visit to Buchenwald, for which concentration camp inmates had to plant flowers and paint their buildings.

Journal columnist John Shaughnessy criticized the law because it "seriously slices into the civil liberties of people in British Columbia without offering heroin addicts realistic prospects of rehabilitation." Most critics similarly reasoned that traditional civil liberties would be denied while the results of this new treatment were unknown.

Although the courts upheld the law, the proposal never went ahead because of public hostility. Recently, it was announced that the center would be changed into a minimum security prison. Jack Altman, one of the last officials to leave the program, said, "only when society learns what works in compulsory treatment will such centers be used."

Alcoholism's coercion laws should be able to avoid such passionate disputes. The new alcoholism procedures have definitely shown they can help at least some alcoholics. Also, reports, especially on TV, have dramatized the alcoholic's confused life, how he or she really wants help though refuses to admit it. This combines with regular broadcasts about alcohol abuse's widespread effects, from hospital costs to highway accidents to criminal violence.

U.S. media have given favorable coverage to the nation's only specialized facility for court-coerced alcoholics. Chronic alcoholics are sent to Pioneer Center North in Washington's Skagit Valley for thirty days, a stay which the court can extend for additional one-month periods up to seven months, most alcoholics remaining three months. The facility has high walls and other security measures. The program's literature notes: "No other treatment facility is equipped to hold persons involuntarily committed. Pioneer has averaged less than one client absconding per month."

Bob Totino, a counselor, describes the program's fifty-five alcoholics as primarily men who "have completely lost control of their ability to handle alcohol, they are often malnourished and suffer from other physical problems brought on by alcoholism." One patient, Jack C., said, "I spent a lot of time in jail, all of it because of alcohol. Every time I got in trouble it was because of alcohol. I couldn't control it. When I was out there, I was nothing."

Pioneer North's administrator, Jim Leake, says, "We were told that if 5 percent of our clients were sober for a month after they left here we could consider ourselves successful." The

Center did a one-year follow-up after it opened in 1979, and Leake admits, "We simply couldn't find the majority of discharged clients," but of the ones contacted, "24.7 percent were leading sober lives" for periods ranging from one month to the full year after discharge.

Janet Page Walthew, who conducted the 1980 interviews, says: "They weren't happy about being here. But in retrospect they can see that they needed more time than they thought. With most of the people I talk with, the issue of involuntary commitment has become less important in retrospect. For many, the freedom of movement lost through involuntary commitment was replaced by freedom from physical addiction to alcohol."

A separate 1981 study of Pioneer's success rate by the Washington State Alcoholism Monitoring System found similar results: 20 to 25 percent of all clients had been continuously sober during the fifteen months following discharge.

Administrator Leake notes the center's "minimum security provisions" are unique. He believes the specialized facility is the best way to treat a legally compelled patient. "It needs to be recognized that most of the clients in this group are white males who have lived alone and been unemployed for a long period of time with essentially no support systems or minimal ones at best. Our success supports the notion that an enforced stay for the chronic alcoholic who has no other resources available to him can be beneficial to that client. Time allows toxicity to decrease so that the client reaches a point where he may make rational decisions in a supportive atmosphere." He adds that a recovered chronic alcoholic saves the public in "food stamps, welfare payments, hospital admissions, detox, county lock-up."

Leake declares that intensive research that follows clients for years is needed to find out which aspects of treatment are most important. He hopes the state will begin "a computerized pre- and post-treatment survey," interviewing all patients at six-month intervals from the time of arrival at the facility and continuing when many return to regular life. "The book on the treatment of alcoholism is still being written."

Increasingly health professionals are analyzing the effectiveness of coercive treatment procedures. Dr. Andrew Abrahams, director of the Bedford-Stuyvesant Alcoholism Treatment Program, says, for example, that he is opposed to compulsory treatment on principle, but "once you have such laws at least make them work. Now I have patients who are dropping out before their treatment is over since they know they'll get their driver's license back."

New York's Department of Motor Vehicles restores the license of an alcoholic referred for therapy unless the treatment facility maintains that the patient has not "reached a level in treatment wherein he would be able to safely operate a motor vehicle on the highways of this State." Clinics, however, generally refuse to write such letters, arguing they are not qualified to judge when a person can drive safely. Alcoholism programs will indicate only whether the coerced patient dropped out prematurely, is still in treatment, or completed therapy. Since these comments don't relate to being a safe driver, New York State's Department of Motor Vehicles has a legal "proof problem," says Richard Smith, highway safety coordinator. As a result, the department routinely reinstates the license of a convicted drunk driver eight months after arrest.

Consequently, many alcoholics leave treatment and just wait for the license to be returned. The alternative is to change the law so that hospital confirmation that the alcoholic driver has completed the prescribed treatment is required before his or her license is returned. This would lead to more patients completing treatment, but such a law also could result in license revocations lasting a month, six months, one year, or perhaps permanently for a treatment drop out, since alcoholics vary greatly in their social and health problems and their ability to accept therapy. Long-term or possible permanent denial of a license is a social and economic hardship. Giving such authority to treatment staffs can lead to patient harassment as well as potential corruption.

This is the kind of issue that will shape the boundaries of

future coercive laws. Others, already noted in this chapter, include: Is the threat of jail appropriate for individuals in family court who never committed a crime? Should a court review a forced treatment procedure before it starts? For example, there is no initial review for the alcoholic who loses his welfare. Does forcing an alcoholic to take a drug like Antabuse violate the Constitution's protection against cruel and inhuman punishment?

How these questions are answered will reveal more than the extent of society's willingness to force alcoholics into treatment. Alcoholism impacts on a significant portion of society. Public discussion about these new coercion laws may also indicate whether the nation is ready to accept coercive treatment for other problems as well.

Dr. Karl Menninger, the psychiatrist, wrote about a future when young criminals are sent on a mass basis to small, residential treatment centers for intensive therapy. First, though, the public must recognize that such youths are sick and need treatment, and then pass the necessary laws, he wrote. Menninger described the procedure in words that are strikingly similar to the principles behind alcoholism's compulsory treatment: "It will surely have to begin with motivating or stimulating or arousing in a coerced individual the wish and hope and intention to change his methods of dealing with the realities of life. Can this be done by education, medication, counseling, training? I would answer *yes*. It can be done in a majority of cases, if undertaken in time."

Dr. Nicholas Kittrie, director of the Institute of Policy and Law at American University Law School and author of the book, *The Right to be Different — Deviance and Enforced Therapy,* comments that: "Five years ago, for example, there was a whole movement for prisoners' rights. You could punish prisoners but not force them to undergo any training, any education, and so on. But recently Chief Justice Warren Burger of the Supreme Court criticized penal institutions, and now his criticism was different. The criticism was that we do not offer these people enough training and enough treatment, enough vocational education. If we do not offer them these particular services how will they get prepared for their return to society?"

New York City's homeless were long protected from coercive treatment procedures. Taking people who were no threat and had committed no crime off the street offended the public's sense of what was right. In 1981, TV and newspapers brought the plight of the homeless to the public's attention, dramatizing their health and security problems. The city, with the tepid approval of the New York Civil Liberties Union, passed a law allowing social service agencies to obtain court orders to force street persons to go to medical facilities for seventy-two hours. After that time, they could leave.

Still, in January 1982, a woman in her late sixties who had lived for eight months in a cardboard box was found frozen to death. The media explained how police and social workers had long known about her living conditions but had failed to invoke the new law. City officials replied that although certain street people appeared vulnerable to harm from criminals or the weather, the law stated that courts could grant permission for the forced seventy-two-hour help only when immediate harm was apparent. "We have to try to do it (first) on a voluntary basis," defended James LoBosco, the director of Protective Services for Adults. "We have to show the court that every effort was made. We're concerned about people's civil rights."

But Kathy Ruby, a city press spokeswoman, later announced that in the future city social workers would not spend so much time on voluntary persuasion. They would go quickly to court for a protective custody order even if no harm was imminent. The courts would be challenged to interpret the law broadly.

Since then, the city discovered a woman living in her car in a poor area of Brooklyn. She was alert enough to park on alternate sides of the street on different days in order to obey parking regulations. The city petitioned for the seventy-two-hour hospitalization, the judge agreed, and doctors found she had gangrene in her toes.

As Coercion Spreads

Because of the importance of public opinion, the early targets of coercion will be primarily drunk drivers and other criminal offenders. Most compulsory measures affect primarily the poor. Consequently, opponents of legal intervention charge that it is discriminatory as well as in violation of civil rights. But, "the alcoholics arrested for drunk driving include executives in three-piece suits as well as laborers with dusty shoes and paint-spattered pants," comments Robert Foley, director of New York City's largest drunk driving program.

Another impetus for focusing first on the drunk driver is because treatment is more effective the earlier it is provided. A study of 140 patients by Dr. Paley of the Long Island Center for Problem Drinking revealed that: "The alcoholic patient who is more likely to complete inpatient treatment seems to be an individual who is seeking help for the first time, who is not a late onset drinker, who has a full-time job, and whose family will be involved in the treatment process. This individual generally will be less than forty years old, live with a family . . ." Younger alcoholics, including teenagers, will be included in coercive treatment programs for arrested drivers. The public is demanding action to curb drunk driving, but fines and even brief jail sentences will not break a person's alcoholism addiction. During the 1970s about a quarter of a million people died from drunk driving. "We're convinced that the single greatest highway safety problem now is the drunk driver," says John Moulden of the National Highway Traffic Administration.

The *New York Times* recently printed the following angry, blunt obituary placed by the deceased's family: "KATZ–Richard. 31. Hit and killed instantly by drunken driver on August 22, 1982."

In addition, a connection between excessive alcohol consumption and other criminal acts has been clearly documented. The Swedish government estimated that 62 percent of all criminals were abusing alcohol when they committed their crime. Nearly one in every two homicides involved severe drunkenness. "If people indulged less in alcohol less often some homicides would never occur," emphasizes Milan Valverius, deputy head of the State Institute of Forensic Medicine in Stockholm. Dr. John Gunn, of London's Institute of Psychiatry, writes, "No matter from which angle the relationship between crime and mental disorder is viewed, the problems of alcoholism always stand out." Dr. Lance Simpson, who teaches psychopharmacology at Columbia University College of Physicians and Surgeons, analyzed Manhattan felonies and found, "When a person commits an act of crime under the influence of a drug, the substance most likely to be involved is alcohol."

Alcohol has a definite link to U.S. crime — 83 percent of prisoners drank before committing their offense, more than 65 percent report personal drinking problems, and 20 percent had at least eight drinks daily in the year before going to jail, according to the NIAAA and Justice Department. A criminal court judge usually has the discretion to offer an alcoholic jail or treatment by writing the choice into an order of probation or conditional discharge. Some states have specific laws concerning diversion. Pennsylvania, for example, authorizes commitment for treatment of up to one year in lieu of a criminal sentence, except in cases of murder. If the convicted alcoholic accepts treatment and then fails to complete it, he or she is sent to prison.

However, criminal judges rarely offer alcoholics the coercive treatment choice. Far more drug offenders than alcoholics are diverted into treatment, points out Vincent Rinella of the Eagleville, Pennsylvania, Hospital and Rehabilitation Center, which treats narcotic addicts and alcoholics. He says: "The intoxicated alcoholic commits more violent or semiviolent crimes against the person than his or her drug-abusing counterpart, who tends to commit crimes against property, often though not always, to obtain money for the purchase of more illicit drugs. The alcoholic offender is often older than the drug-abusing defendant, which may produce a feeling of hopelessness regarding his or her chances for obtaining a diversionary disposition."

However, an Eagleville study, which compared success rates for alcohol and narcotic abusing offenders diverted into treatment, found that alcoholics "do as well or even better than drug abusers." Thomas Epstein, an attorney with the School of Public Health at the University of California in Berkeley, argues that an alcoholic is an ill person, unable to control his drinking, so if he commits a crime related to his drunkenness he should be found not guilty. He wants to change the present law, which does not allow a person's alcoholism to be a defense to a crime but considers it only in reducing the punishment, and so this offender can be ordered to select prison or treatment.

If this not-guilty alcoholic is arrested for another crime related to intoxication, Epstein reasons, then the alcoholism defense could be denied by the jury, since the defendant previously had been legally warned about the consequences of his drinking. At this time, a judge could offer the choice of therapy or jail. But is this the procedure most needed by a crime-besieged public or the alcoholic?

East German law permits a judge to offer an alcoholic criminal probation with treatment in lieu of incarceration. If the offender refuses the therapy and then "commits another offense he will receive an aggravated degree of punishment," comments Dr. Hans Hinderer of Martin Luther University in Halle. Should America accept this use of extra punishment as a coercive threat? It could open the way to severely penalizing a defendant who failed to correct a variety of behaviors — unemployment, not having a fixed address, not attending school — that a court advised him to change.

At a recent conference, Florida County Court Judge John Shannon said he always uses coercive treatment for alcoholics who haven't committed serious felonies and often requires that they take Antabuse if accepting this probation offer. Shannon, a recovered alcoholic, believes the importance of coercive treatment is starting to be recognized by judges. The more state laws passed on diverting alcoholic criminals into therapy, the more judicial attention will be focused on coercion's possibilities, he notes.

County outpatient facilities in San Francisco now receive half of their patients from criminal court referrals, according to a study by Connie Weisner of the Medical Research Institute of San Francisco. The crimes include petty larceny, drunk driving, assault and battery, and prostitution.

Favorable international experiences are also influential in this area. South Africa's high success rate with forced treatment involves criminals significantly, emphasizes A.J. Auret, Director General of the Department of Health, Welfare and Pensions. "An average of 47 percent of men sent for compulsory treatment to state rehabilitation centers during 1980 were admitted by the Criminal Procedures Act of 1977."

Belgium reports increasing use of compulsory treatment for criminals, and 7 percent of the alcoholics in treatment in New Zealand were coerced there by the criminal court. Portuguese judges can order alcoholic criminals, after they serve their sentence, into special prison treatment facilities for six months to three years. Dr. J. Gerchow of Goethe University in Frankfurt says, "It is discernible that authorities increasingly embrace this aspect of coercion, and alcoholics having become criminally liable therefore have an increasingly better chance for treatment."

The public, of course, expects success from coercive treatment, for whatever group of alcoholics. As Robin Room, of the University of California School of Public Health at Berkeley, warns, "The natural history of treatment movements for intractable problems in the U.S. is for a period of expansion, high hopes, and extravagant claims of success to be succeeded by a period of retrenchment, pessimism, and clinical nihilism."

Since alcoholism's compulsory treatment efforts have shown that they can restore alcoholics to health, they should not have to join the list of interesting failures in health texts. But if these laws do prove unable to help sizeable numbers of people, then the public might support a backlash. The recent study, *Alcohol and Public Policy,* by a National Research Council panel brought up the possibility of seeking out working alcoholics before they ever display problems on the job: "This approach undoubtedly raises serious issues of civil liberty, but the pros and cons of the 'intrusion' must be weighed. Checks can be applied in an objective and nondiscriminatory manner, using, for example, a breathalyzer for all personnel with certain responsibilities. Although the check-in may be regarded as odious, the occupational safety rationale should make it more acceptable. Clearly it would be a message about the hazards of certain jobs, a warning to those who know that they drink excessively, and a communication that drunkenness will not be covered up or implicitly condoned in jobs in which certain risks are involved. Specific identification of such jobs is not a task that this panel has undertaken, but categories such as air traffic and flight control, missile guidance, heavy crane operation, surgery, and medical intensive care come to mind. More generally, 36 percent of the labor force in 1971 was engaged in work involving a fairly complex relationship to 'things' (i.e., machines, tools, equipment, products), and 15 percent of all the occupations listed in the *Dictionary of Occupational Titles* involve working under hazardous conditions."

In his well-known text for teaching social workers, *Alcoholism — Challenge for Social Work Education,* Herman Krimmel points out that he wanted to include examples of government and court intervention with alcoholics in addition to his many case illustrations of how therapists counsel patients. When writing this book in 1971, he found few examples of public intervention, an "imbalance in favor of the individual approach."

Krimmel emphasized, "Alcoholism, like other social problems cannot be eradicated, or even significantly diminished, by the exclusive use of this method (helping one person or one family). It will only succumb to social action resulting in basic social change."

Now, a decade later, with the growth of coercive treatment laws, that potential social action has appeared.

Confronting the Alcoholic

This chapter began with a call from someone living with an alcoholic, from someone who felt overwhelmed, desperately overwhelmed. "*Please,* get the police, get anyone to take him for help. He's killing himself, he's killing us."

While the new compulsory treatment laws can bring many more addicted drinkers into therapy, their scope is still limited. The alcoholic must have a criminal or family court problem or be on welfare.

The 30 million wives, children, lovers, friends, and other relatives who live with alcoholics who will not be helped by these measures should consider "nonlegal" confrontation. Its goal is to overwhelm the alcoholic's ability to explain why he doesn't need help, overwhelm the defense system that justifies his drinking. He has told himself that he knows/feels that only with alcohol's euphoria is he happy, and why shouldn't he have the right to be happy? How can anyone live each day without some reward system that cries, "You're good. Hell, yes, you think and feel and understand. If only the others had some of your sensitivity."

When someone tries to tell the drinker that alcohol is wrecking his and his family's life, the defense system springs to life. He *denies:* "You're wrong, I never said that at the party. Maybe it was you who had too many there." He *rationalizes:* "If you knew my pressures at work. That's why I needed to unwind that night and so I missed the kid's game, but it'll be different when the new supervisor is hired." He *blames:* "If you were a loving woman, I wouldn't have to drink so much."

To force the alcoholic to be honest with himself — about what really is happening to his life, about how unhappy he really is — the family member must maintain a consistently honest approach toward the alcoholic's drinking. Honesty does not mean shrilly blaming the alcoholic for not controlling his drinking, causing him to feel more misunderstood and guilty and possibly to drink more. Honesty does require that the family stop protecting the alcoholic from recognizing his behavior.

For example, a friend calls about going out. John has a hangover or has injured himself while drunk. The wife should have John talk to the caller or, if he can't, tell the friend that they are unable to make the date but John will phone soon to explain why. John may then mumble a lie into the phone, but he will be forced to feel how drinking is causing him discomfort.

Wanting to protect her husband from embarrassment, the wife instead may say, "I'm sorry, but we have another appointment," or "John has a bad cold." This cover-up makes her husband's as well as her own life more comfortable, but it prevents the alcoholic from recognizing how he is being harmed by alcohol.

The cover-up instinct becomes difficult to control with the following call: "This is John's boss, and he called to say he was sick and I wanted to phone to ask how he is." John is now passed out or so high that he may say something inappropriate. The best response is the honest one, especially if the alcoholic works for a company that has a formal employee alcoholism program. It is usually the largest corporations that have such assistance efforts, however, while the average American works for a small employer, who, if he learns that John has a drinking problem, may fire him.

Rather than lying for John, the wife can tell such a supervisor that her husband will call back by a certain time — sooner than John would choose, before his denial system will be fully alert and believing itself. During this return call, John will worry whether his boss may detect the truth; he may begin to realize that he may lose his job because of his drinking.

In addition to establishing a consistent attitude toward the alcoholic, the nonalcoholic spouse should keep a diary of the incidents caused by her drinking: she was the only mother who didn't attend the class meeting; she forgot to pick up her daughter at dance class; she fell asleep and dropped a lighted cigarette on the rug.

With this information and professional assistance the nonalcoholic can stage a confrontation. One source of assistance is the local council of the National Council on Alcoholism, listed in the phone book. With the professional's advice, and usually presence, the confrontation begins. The alcoholic hears about the many incidents, too many for her to deny or rationalize away. The discussion purposely questions the alcoholic about how she *feels*.

"Because of these work absences, you may get fired and then we wouldn't have enough money to keep living here. How do you feel about that?" "The kids told you they refuse to bring home friends because you don't get dressed properly. Does that concern you?" "You not only almost killed yourself but also your son when you wrecked the car. How does that make you feel?"

"Yes, I feel bad. No, I don't like to feel bad. But listen, if I lived in a warmer climate, I wouldn't feel so lousy. If the kids didn't watch so much TV, they'd have more respect. If Detroit built safer cars . . ."

The family member and professional, however, keep making the alcoholic realize that *each* of these incidents resulted from drinking. If you drink, this is what will continue to happen, how you will continue to feel. Do you want to feel happier?

The professional explains that alcoholism is an illness. He may compare it to an allergy. Why do some people suffer severe reactions to certain foods while others feel nothing? It's not the allergic person's fault. There's no blame. But once realizing that he has an allergy, the individual can continue to feel terrible or get help.

If the alcoholic now agrees to try treatment, the professional will recommend either that he or she go regularly to Alcoholics Anonymous meetings, or, usually, first receive more intensive medical therapy and then enroll with AA.

Alcoholism treatment consists of supportive therapy, most often done through a sharing, group process. During these sessions the alcoholic realizes how he was destroying his own and his loved ones' lives and how this damage can keep getting worse. The therapy helps the alcoholic recognize that he can't drink without harm — yet that he has the strength to get through each day without booze's anesthesia.

Reflecting on her alcoholism, Betty Ford explained that even Washington's public spotlight could not force her to admit to herself how alcohol was hurting her life. She needed a planned confrontation to recognize the need for treatment:

> I never thought I needed treatment. I was like any alcoholic; everybody else was at fault, not me. I think intervention is valuable. It can be the most life-saving approach there is. To be able to intervene or to confront somebody at a point of their alcoholic progression before they cause themselves irreparable bodily harm is a big step forward in the recovery process. This is when a chemically dependent person should come into treatment and learn how to cope with their addiction. They don't have all the medical complications that come later, the physical disabilities that can develop with chronic addiction. In fact, we are being unfair if we *don't* intervene with people. It is a question of how to do it successfully, and I think it is best done with the aid of a professional who truly understands intervention.

6

An Alcoholism Test?

The ultimate way to confront and treat alcoholism would be to identify people who are predisposed to this illness and make their bodies resistant to alcohol addiction before they ever drink. This long-discussed prevention dream now has a chance of becoming a reality.

Researchers increasingly believe that alcoholics are born with a physical susceptibility to alcohol. This weakness tends to be restrained in a society that restricts consumption or released in one where heavy drinking is common. A person who cannot resist stress well, has this physical predisposition, and lives in a drinking society is especially prone to become an alcoholic, according to the present theories on the cause of this illness.

The most frequently cited study supporting the existence of an inherited susceptibility was done by Donald Goodwin of the University of Kansas Medical Center. Goodwin reviewed the records of 110 adopted children in Denmark from the time they were adopted, at the age of six weeks, until they were ages twenty-five to twenty-nine. Twenty percent of the children whose natural parents were alcoholic became alcoholics themselves, while only 5 percent of the other adopted children eventually suffered from alcoholism. (None of the 110 sets of adoptive parents were alcoholic.)

Cell Membranes Yield A Clue

Efforts to identify this physical predisposition have spawned many theories, but the work now considered the most promising involves cell membrane research, focusing on alcohol's effect on the lining that covers the cell. Yedy Israel of the Canadian Addiction Research Foundation and the University of Toronto says that a common factor in all nerve cells is the production and propagation of electrical currents in the membrane. Alcohol inhibits this process, says Israel, citing recent studies that show that when alcohol becomes dissolved in the cell membrane, the physical and chemical properties of the membrane become altered and disorganized.

Working with this theory, Dora Goldstein of Stanford University Medical Center found that when alcohol travels through the blood to the brain, the membranes of the brain cells become soft and unstable, with the molecules moving around as if heated. She then fed alcohol to mice until they developed tolerance, the condition whereby over time an addict requires more and more of the drug to achieve the desired high. The brain cell membranes in tolerant or alcohol-addicted mice were more resistant to the effects of alcohol than those in the nonaddicted "regular drinkers" group. Because of this resistance, the tolerant animals required increasingly larger doses of alcohol in order to be satisfied.

A higher level of cholesterol was found to be the cause of the alcohol resistance in the tolerant group's membranes. Goldstein's research has increased practical value because she also observed higher cholesterol levels in the red blood cells of the tolerant mice.

Alcoholism researchers can visualize the day when children with family histories of alcoholism will automatically take blood tests to determine if their cell membranes are the type that become tolerant to alcohol. If the test is positive, the youths will receive both injections and a special diet to regulate the cholesterol level of their cell membranes so that they will be able to avoid alcohol addiction. The youngsters' bodies will then react to alcohol in the same way as nonalcoholics: they may become drunk but not alcoholic.

Dr. Anne Geller, of St. Luke's-Roosevelt Hospital in New

York, sees a future when "we'll deal with alcoholism in the same way we test the youngster with a family record of diabetes. If positive, we then give him insulin injections and a new diet to control the illness."

"Modification of membrane lipids by dietary fatty acids or injected phospholipid vesicles can now be envisioned and is currently the subject of very active research," says Goldstein. She is unable to predict when this might become routine medical procedure, although much has happened in cell membrane research in just the last ten years. She can foresee "a stage where physicians might be able to monitor and manipulate the state of membrane fluidity of their patients as routinely as they now control a patient's electrolyte balance."

Supporting Goldstein's findings is Boris Tabakoff of the Department of Physiology and Biophysics at the University of Illinois Medical Center. Tabakoff, who has conducted his own research into finding the genetic fault that alcoholics inherit, says, "Goldstein's and other studies have provided strong support for the contention that ethanol sensitivity is genetically determined and, to a great extent, due to the composition of an animal's or a person's neuronal membranes. The search for this understanding and other ethanol-related effects will, in the end, provide for us the proper tools for treating and preventing alcoholism."

"The future will see a genetic test to identify the pre-alcoholic, and the question is just what it'll look like and when we'll perfect it," says Dr. Sheila Blume, medical director of the National Council on Alcoholism.

Not Guilty by Reason of Alcoholism

A blood test distinguishing the alcoholic from the simply intoxicated drinker would rewrite headlines such as those of the Abscam criminal trials. Congressmen John Jenrette of South Carolina and Michael Meyers of Pennsylvania argued that they had been too intoxicated to understand what they were doing and that this condition was caused by alcoholism. A little later, Congressman Robert Bauman of Maryland offered the same "not responsible" defense in a sex offense case.

The courts rejected their pleas. Accepting them would have meant dramatic changes in the nation's criminal laws to add the defense of "not guilty by reason of alcoholism," just as courts now allow the "not guilty by reason of mental illness" argument, with the defendant entering a treatment facility instead of jail until the condition is cured.

Future research could allow courts to distinguish addicted offenders with alcohol-tolerant membranes from defendants who committed their acts while intoxicated. When such a distinction becomes possible, and when cell membrane tests are routinely run on drunken offenders, the defense of not guilty by reason of alcoholism could become legally accepted. As a result, more people would enter treatment since more than 60 percent of all prisoners report drinking problems.

Vast Benefits Despite a Drawback

A new wave of drug abuse may follow such successful addiction prevention, warns Blume, since many of the "cured" potential alcoholics might still have a psychological need to maintain a high. Many of today's drinkers have discovered the magnified euphoria obtained by mixing alcohol with barbiturates, amphetamines, and marijuana. Alcoholics Anonymous states that 45 percent of its members under thirty are now abusing drugs other than alcohol. Present drug addicts demand emotional relief more quickly than did their predecessors, according to numerous studies.

The danger is that potential alcoholics will receive cholesterol manipulation of their cells but not the intensive therapy of alcoholism treatment that teaches individuals how to deal with stress. These persons can then be expected to seek out and abuse drugs other than alcohol and become addicted to other chemicals that provide quick relief from tension. On the other hand, California psychopharmacologist Ronald Siegel has optimistically noted that he can foresee the eventual production of a synthetic formula to create a sense of well-being without leaving its takers suffering from a damaging psychological or physical addiction. To achieve this, Siegel said, "we need to learn more about chemical pathways and the ways of providing stimulations for these pathways in the safest possible ways." This knowledge gap could be filled in large part by the advancing research on how alcohol distorts the brain cell passages through which nerve impulses flow.

Being able to stop the progression of alcoholism would yield incredible advantages. The already known benefits are enormous: U.S. health statistics list alcoholic liver cirrhosis as the sixth leading cause of death, and Canadian health officials predict that it will be their number three killer by 1985. Controlling alcoholism would immediately save New York City $1.1 billion annually, according to estimates by the city's Department of Mental Health. National savings would include $20 billion lost to industry by absent and inefficient workers, $13 billion for medical and hospital treatment, and $2 billion in welfare payments. These financial gains for society fade when compared to the years and often lifetimes of human misery that would be avoided by persons born with an inherited alcoholism sensitivity.

7

The Ethics of It All

Should Americans readily accept the practice of taking blood to identify children who may have been born with a genetic weakness for alcoholism? Would government gain access to this hospital information and then monitor the lives of youths with positive tests? And if these persons began to abuse alcohol, what would the watching officials do?

Previous chapters discussed the government regulations, awareness campaigns, and support of new research that can moderate the consumption of alcohol as well as pressure legally competent alcoholics to get therapy. Could such actions, intervening to change a lifestyle as well the decision on whether to seek help to save one's life, open the way for bureaucrats to overwhelm many individual rights in the name of better health? Will Americans wish they had never tried to eliminate their worst drug problem? What protections can be established *now* that will allow achievement of the immense human and financial rewards without contributing to the kind of society that civil rights advocates have long feared and that Plato idealized in his *Republic*? There the ruler was a benevolent doctor (read also all-powerful government agency, courts, and scientists) who was given the right to direct people's lives since he understood what was best for them.

The potential to move in this direction is great. If society forces certain groups to change their lives, the public benefits would be enormous. "As much as 50 percent of mortality from the ten leading causes of death in the United States can be traced to lifestyle," concluded a recent study by the Institute of Medicine of the National Academy of Science. "Known behavioral risk factors include cigarette smoking, excessive consumption of alcohol, use of illicit drugs, certain dietary habits, reckless driving, nonadherence to effective medication regimens and maladaptive responses to social pressures . . . There is an unprecedented opportunity in prevention and therapy."

Americans need to make their opinions known about the protections they want in these new measures. The obvious area where the public could take its first stand is compulsory treatment, since these procedures are already affecting the rights of hundreds of thousands of people. What safeguards can be written into these regulations that would protect the rights of the individual while still allowing the laws to stop alcohol's havoc? Once this priority is publicly established in the compulsory procedures, it will likely be reflected in the other actions that aim at curtailing excessive drinking and alcoholism.

Help or Harm

Any ethical review of a government procedure must first look at the people being affected, and their acceptance or resistance. Consider, for example, a man, convicted of drunk driving, who angrily entered my office not long ago to complain that he had been "tricked." In court he had agreed to attend a seven-week alcohol education class at the nonprofit agency that I direct. In return his fine would be reduced by $100 and his license returned when the program ended rather than after six months.

By New York law, each class participant was interviewed to determine whether he had had only a few too many before driving or suffered from a psychological or physical addiction that left him unable to control his drinking. Those identified as alcoholic — about 25 percent of the class — were referred to an outpatient hospital clinic for therapy. There they participated in group counseling sessions once a week for about ten months. The purpose of these sessions was to help them gain the self-strength needed to give up drinking completely. If a driver refused to take this treatment, his license could remain suspended (although, as noted earlier, the Motor Vehicles Department routinely returns a license after eight months, even if the alcoholic refuses therapy).

The folder of this angry man — Joel, a stockbroker — was on my desk. I explained to him that he experienced blackouts or loss of memory when drinking; he had received warnings from his supervisor about poor sales, which he himself admitted had fallen "from too much time boozing"; and he had an increasingly strained relationship with his wife who kept berating him to stop drinking.

"But I promise you I'll cut back, way back soon. I'll do it myself. Don't make me go for treatment." His voice became loud as he expressed his fear that once he entered a hospital program someone he knew would see him, and his boss and neighbors would find out he was alcoholic.

I assured Joel that attendance at a clinic was confidential information by law. If anyone called there, the treatment staff could not even say they knew Joel.

He kept arguing: "They'll think I'm a no-good. Someone you can't trust. Listen, I'll sign something that if I can't stop drinking soon by myself, I'll go to a hospital then. Say in four months. Anyway, if they find out then, they'll see I did it myself. I'm a responsible person. Come on, don't report me to Motor Vehicles. I need my license back."

I said I realized that the public mistakenly saw the alcoholic as a weak person who could stop drinking if only he wanted to, rather than as someone suffering from an addiction and needing therapy. The fear of giving up this drug has earned alcoholism the name of "the disease of denial." Few alcoholics, only about one in seven, ever go for help willingly. That is why the drunk-driver laws in most states require the alcoholics arrested to get counseling immediately.

Joel suddenly rose from his chair. A big man in a three-piece suit, he looked at me, looked angrily into me, and then just walked out of my office.

Joel had been caught up by the growing number of coercive treatment laws that threaten alcoholics with various penalties, fines, and even jail sentences if they fail to get help. As Jerauld D. Miller, publisher of the magazine *Alcoholism* and a recovered alcoholic, recently wrote in an editorial: "No more than 15 percent (of the nation's 10 million alcoholics) will seek treatment on their own. But if America were to declare an unlimited war on drunk driving, meting out mandatory treatment for the more than 700,000 alcoholics convicted of DWI (Driving While Intoxicated) each year, we could bolster these recovery statistics in championship form."

As discussed in chapter 5, these laws operate not only on drunk drivers but also on welfare recipients, criminal offenders, and alcoholics involved in family court disputes because of their drinking. "People don't realize how extensive this coercion is," says Robin Room, director of the Alcohol Research Group at the University of California at Berkeley. "Even if great numbers of new people are being made to get help, do we want these laws? Sure, I can see the arguments for them. But I'm a person more than a technician. I worry what these laws mean for society generally. We need to determine the limits on them as soon as possible."

Noting that almost half the people in the San Francisco area attending outpatient clinics for alcoholism therapy were pressured by criminal courts to go there through the threat of prison, Richard Spiegelman and Connie Weisner, colleagues of Room at Berkeley, wrote, "One of the most striking elements of the evolving relationship between criminal justice and the alcohol treatment systems is the fact that providers have not really begun to discuss the philosophical issues."

Meanwhile pressure is on legislators and courts to use coercion. The more alcoholics entering therapy, the greater society's chance to significantly reduce its costliest and most extensive drug addiction. After "voluntary" treatment, the chance of staying abstinent or having a significantly improved life ranges from 32 to 68 percent for persons with families and job experience according to the federal government. The less years drinking and so physical and social damage, the greater the chance of treatment success. Court orders can also lead to sobriety for poor, transient alcoholics, although their average recovery rates go downward from 18 percent, since they must often return to life's stress without the aid of a stable home life or daily job.

A 1982 report by the Boston University Medical Center of people with drinking problems confirmed, as countless other studies have, the resistance of alcoholics to enter therapy, to give up what makes their lives bearable. In the Boston survey, 67 percent of the people who had experienced alcohol-caused problems admitted they were conscious of these behaviors before age thirty. Eighty-five percent did not go for treatment when they first recognized these troubles. They said they had believed "their problem was not sufficiently serious and that they could handle it on their own," notes Ralph Hingson of the Boston Center.

When public procedures are designed to overcome resistance of individuals, ethical conflicts are created. Dr. Veronique Bähler, director of an alcoholism treatment program in Geneva, Switzerland, says, "Oh, I am sure that if you get tough enough legal penalties and long enough treatment, you will get more recovered alcoholics. But do you really want such laws? It's a question of ethics, no?"

On the other hand, many recovered alcoholics openly say, "Why did I wait so long, suffer so?" A frustrated social worker from the Charleston, South Carolina, Veterans Administration Hospital recently complained to me about the lack of a law to make the many alcoholic Vietnam Vets, whom she saw for other health problems, go for drinking therapy. Each day countless spouses and children of alcoholics bitterly and sadly ask why society refuses to make the problem drinkers they live with take treatment.

To what extent is the active alcoholic's refusal to willingly go for treatment a personal right that society should protect?

As S. F. Sapontzis, associate professor of philosophy at California State University, has written: "Determining what is morally acceptable and preferable one must take into account what will dignify or demean, benefit or harm, please or pain, aid or thwart, satisfy or dissatisfy, enrich or impoverish, and so forth *any* (emphasis added) person likely to be affected."

The case of Rowena when compared to the story of Joel illustrates the often conflicting attitudes of alcoholics toward therapy. Rowena was a thirty-year-old unmarried mother on welfare, who had given birth to a mentally retarded child. Doctors at Jacobi Hospital in the Bronx diagnosed this retardation as fetal alcohol syndrome, caused by the mother's heavy drinking during pregnancy. They reported the case as a child abuse offense to the city's Child Welfare Bureau, which notified the Welfare Department because Rowena had been on assistance since 1969 when she gave birth to a son, now thirteen.

The baby was placed in foster care, and Rowena was told that because of the child abuse she would not get custody until she went for alcohol treatment. Rowena did nothing for six and a half months. Then she received the notice from the Welfare Department stating that she was an alcoholic and would be cut off from assistance unless she went to a clinic.

Rowena, who looked like a teenager, said she did not believe she was an alcoholic, despite the fetal alcohol syndrome diagnosis, but she now was ready to accept treatment because she wanted her baby back and could not risk losing the welfare payments for her son and herself. Rowena's calm words revealed no anger. Asked if having to go for treatment that she did not think was necessary was a denial of her freedom, Rowena smiled and said, "Oh, no. I don't mind. Let me just do it."

Rowena did admit as the conversation proceeded that when depressed she usually bought a bottle of liquor and consumed it. She also said she had not been able to stop this binge drinking when pregnant.

Alice Petropoulos, the director of the counseling service of the National Council on Alcoholism's New York office, said afterward that Rowena's quiet acceptance of the treatment order was typical for an alcoholic on welfare. "They are used to being told what to do. They also don't have much to lose if someone finds out they are in treatment. That is unlike the arrested drivers we see, who usually are working and have jobs, friends, and family, and worry what they'll think."

Rowena dutifully left for treatment at a city alcoholism clinic. Without the social supports of a regular job or stable family life to return to, the chances of Rowena becoming permanently sober were low, about one in six. Yet there would be no chance if she did not go for this therapy.

Individual Rights Theory

Can the Welfare Department's threat which sent Rowena into treatment satisfy an ethical standard that gives priority to individual rights? This value is based on the belief that a life-style determined by free choice is preferable to a seemingly more rewarding one obtained through outside intervention. Through free will an individual develops his self-worth, and as a result is a healthier more productive person than one who depends on others for direction.

The goal of ethics is to protect the person's autonomy, writes David A. Richards, professor of law at New York University. He defines autonomy as including the "capacities of persons which enable them to develop, want to act on, and act on higher order plans of action." Treatment tries to prevent an alcoholic from continuing to deny recognizing what is happening to his life, and builds up his individual capacities so he can get well. On the other hand, if this therapy results from a legal order, the alcoholic himself did not "act," at least not initially.

Professor Richards, in an example analogous to the alcoholic, questions the ethical right to intervene therapeutically in the life of a person who has a psychosis like kleptomania in which "a present compulsion cannot be resisted though it conflicts with other desires of the agent, both now and in the future, which the agent (may well) deem more important."

The leading advocate of an individual rights-based legal system was, of course, the German philosopher Immanuel Kant. In defining his "conception of Right" in 1796, he pointed out: "Acts of Will or voluntary Choice are thus regarded only in so far as they are *free*, and as to whether the action of one can harmonize with the Freedom of Another, according to a universal law."

Threatened with a termination of her welfare checks as well as the loss of her baby, was Rowena really "free" to reject treatment? The coercive procedure also denied Rowena the freedom eventually to choose help voluntarily. However, since Rowena's drinking harmed her child and its autonomy, this addiction was not in harmony with the "Freedom of Another." A person must stop damaging another's individuality before he can claim his own personal rights. Thus a proponent of individual rights could support the procedure that coerced Rowena into counseling.

"Alcoholics, like any other citizen, have a right to use and abuse alcohol," comments Thomas Perrin, chairman of the New Jersey Task Force on Children of Alcoholics. "When their right to abuse alcohol interferes with the rights of others ... the rights of others take a legitimate precedence. Alcohol intervention isn't a punishment. It's a lifesaving procedure for both abuser and victim."

Another Ethical Theory

The public's rights should also be considered. Is it fair to burden society with the costs of supporting Rowena's drinking, which leaves her unable to work and reliant on welfare? Her alcoholism also has produced a brain-damaged child, whose institutional support will become society's burden.

Balancing the harm to the individual from compulsory

therapy against the benefits to society leads to the other major theory of legal ethics, utilitarianism, whose two great supporters were the Englishmen Jeremy Bentham and John Stuart Mill. Bentham, who died in 1832, wrote: "If the partisan of the *principle of utility* finds in the common lists of virtues an action from which there results more pain than pleasure, he does not hesitate to regard that pretended virtue as a vice."

If protecting an alcoholic's autonomy will result in damage to other people and the general welfare, then society should override this right. The U.S. legal system usually has relied on utilitarian thinking in cases that involve the public good, permitting courts to uphold such acts as the required vaccination of school children, the military draft, and involuntary institutional commitment for the mentally disordered person who is in danger of severely harming himself or others.

In the 1927 case of *Buck* v. *Bell,* which has been strongly criticized by advocates of individual rights, the Supreme Court noted that: "The public welfare may call upon the best citizens for their lives. It would be strange if it could not call upon those who already sap the strength of the State for these lesser sacrifices, often not felt to be such by those concerned." The case upheld the state of Virginia's right to sterilize a "feeble-minded white woman." Adopting a utilitarian standard for alcoholism's new compulsory treatment laws would leave those affected with the least protection.

Writing and interpreting the coercion procedures through a utilitarian view focuses on the simpler question of whether or not society is being harmed and allows judges and government agencies to avoid recognizing the differing reactions of alcoholics caught up in these orders. Some persons, like Joel, can claim they are being harmed by the procedures; others, like Rowena, will not oppose intervention; and some alcoholics may embrace this mandated help.

Terry is an example from this last group of alcoholics. He was very emotional about the drunk driver arrest that forced him to attend an alcohol education class, but it was emotion filled with gratitude. In his late twenties, Terry said that because of these classes he now realized his father was an alcoholic and that he was especially at risk to become one, since drinking problems ran in his family. Terry said he intended to cut down significantly on his drinking. He had not had a drink in four months when I talked with him.

"You know, like I'm going to my sister-in-law's shower next week," he said. "I might have really put one on in the past. But now I know I won't. I'll just have one, if that. I realize how I acted before. How I slurred my words. What I must have been like. No, I don't want that no more."

Terry, who works as a teacher's aide at a school for the mentally retarded, said: "I just wish the penalties were more severe so the first time I was arrested I would have gone into this program and not waited. The stiffer the penalties the better. I'm a new person, believe me, I never felt so good. Thankfully I got the help before it was too late."

The diversity among alcoholics will cause those concerned with preventing oversights in the sensitive area of regulating people's behavior to write laws according to an individual rights — rather than utilitarian — framework, including specific protections responsive to the many different kinds of persons and situations affected. Such visible expression of public sentiment is important because otherwise legislators and judges only know that society already practices extensive intervention with alcoholics and so might not desire special protective clauses when government performs this same intervention.

Employers now tell alcoholics to go for treatment or risk losing jobs. Therapists teach the nonalcoholic spouse to say, "Go for help or I and the kids will leave to protect our own health."

Sharon Wegscheider, president of a family consulting group in Minneapolis, trains families on how to keep diaries of the alcoholics' negative behaviors and then confront them with these facts. "When any of us is sincerely concerned about chemical abuse and lets the person know it, we are intervening," says Wegscheider. "Intervention can take place

between family members and the alcoholic, or between professionals and family members."

Maureen Denham-Hainsy, an alcoholism therapist with
Portland's Burnside Project, says the program practices coercion with skid-row and welfare alcoholics without waiting for
legal procedures. "We refuse to rescue. We say we will help *if*
the person goes to detox (a seven-day hospital stay to remove
the alcohol out of the individual) or goes to treatment (inpatient, lasting a month or more)." Co-worker Peter Barrios
adds, "Or gets involved in the patient program with monitored
Antabuse and monitored Alcoholics Anonymous." Offering
help in this fashion, Barrios says, creates "the breadcrumb
trail."

Alcoholic therapy tries to make the drinker completely
surrender to the fact that he or she can never drink, rather than
comply, which counselors define as believing he or she will be
able to handle alcohol in the future. Alina Lodge, in Blairs-
town, New Jersey, one of the best-known treatment programs,
notifies patients before they enter that its philosophy "is a
nonpermissive approach to the treatment of alcoholism and
addiction. The program is geared to assisting the alcoholic to
use self-discipline in all his/her behaviors both here and in the
future. Structured living is a strong support in this goal."

Ethical Limits

Despite the regular practice of therapeutic coercion in
industry and the rigid nature of treatment, people working in
alcoholism are not ready to completely support government
intervention in the affairs of alcoholics. A survey of thirty-six
government health officials and alcohol treatment directors
from sixteen nations conducted by me as chairman of the legal
issues section of the International Council on Alcohol and
Addictions revealed that these individuals would not support
all mandatory measures and that they largely used an individual rights test in determining their opinions. Table 1 presents
a statistical summary of the survey results (see Appendix A).

Sixty-one percent of those polled supported laws that threaten an alcoholic on welfare with a cutoff of support if he fails to go for treatment. The survey responses, however, were equally divided about whether a court should order treatment for the alcoholic who is involved in a family dispute but has violated no law. Yet there is a two to three times greater chance of successfully treating alcoholics who still have families than the welfare poor who often lack steady social supports. In addition, the alcoholic can severely damage his or her family, creating permanent emotional harm and leaving children unable to function fully. "At an early age, they [children of alcoholics] are trapped in a self-destructive cycle of despair and failure that ruins their lives and harms the society of which they are part," New York's former governor Hugh Carey said, following a 1982 study of this problem.

Analyzing family violence cases in Finland, Teuvo Peltoniemi reported that, "One of the main issues in 60 percent of home disputes leading to violence was said to be alcohol and the unwillingness of the partner to seek help for alcohol problems when suggested by the victim." One abused wife told Peltoniemi: "But there is a subject he does not want to talk about at all. And that is alcohol, just that."

The international survey favored regulations that coerce the public assistance recipient but not laws for alcohol abusers involved in family disputes, indicating that the principle of utilitarianism — measuring how much a group damages society — was not followed. The survey's participants instead gave priority to individual rights. Protecting the sanctity of the home and the individual's behavior in it is strongly valued as a personal right; someone's qualification to receive public assistance is not.

Could this strong sentiment toward family privacy possibly need legal protection one day? In 1971, Delaware became the first state to allow a family court judge to order an alcoholic parent to take treatment or risk a heavy fine or jail sentence. At the many national conferences on alcoholism that discussed this law, the clear sentiment was that no other state would adopt such a regulation. Affecting alcoholics who had committed no legal wrong, this coercion-into-treatment law went too far.

In July 1982, however, Tom Kean, governor of New Jersey, signed a new family court act. The law states that when a court has a "juvenile in crisis" — meaning a youth committed a crime, ran away from home, or failed to attend school regularly — and when a parent's alcoholism contributed to this situation, the judge can order this father or mother to accept treatment or be in contempt of court and face a jail sentence or fine.

"A group of mothers and wives of alcoholics had learned about the Delaware law and were responsible for putting in this provision," says David Evans, the attorney for New Jersey's Division of Alcoholism. "Their urging made the state do a study, in a town of 30,000 near Philadelphia, of kids who committed crimes. It turned out about twenty families were responsible for 93 percent of the offenses, and sixteen of these families had one or two alcoholic parents. Another survey in a different town, of kids under eighteen who got into frequent police problems, found 25 percent had an alcoholic parent . . . So while no one in New Jersey originally wanted to intervene with families, we finally decided to do it. There was no opposition to this coercive treatment procedure when the governor signed the bill."

New York State officials have long resisted coercing into clinics alcoholic parents involved in family court disputes in which there has been no physical child abuse. A family court provision that went into effect in August 1981 involving orders of protection, where spouses physically threaten each other or their children, allows the court only to order the offender to "participate in an educational program" concerning his emotional, drug, or alcohol problem. Treatment specifically is not included.

Yet a year later the state report on children of alcoholics discovered for itself what was long known about the effects of living in an alcoholic home: these youths "often do poorly in school and are frequently truant or delinquent." The study proposed allowing family court judges to compel an alcoholic parent into treatment or deny him child custody.

In the sixteen-nation survey, an individual rights view was also found in the question about coercive treatment for prisoners. Ninety-three percent said that an alcoholic criminal who chooses treatment as a condition of probation or parole should be given the most effective therapy, even if it lasts longer than the alternative jail sentence.

Coming primarily from unstable living conditions as well as having education and employment problems, criminals are a difficult group of alcoholics to treat. The success rate in achieving abstinence will be low, in line with the 18 percent or less recovery rate for the transient poor. The recommendation to offer extended treatment could result in costs that exceed the benefits to society.

"Prisoners who used alcohol at the time of the crime were educationally deprived and unemployed at a higher rate than prisoners who had not used alcohol," comments Gisela Spieker, based on her study of convicts who were alcohol abusers; 69 percent had not completed tenth grade and 66 percent were unemployed.

At present, courts and prison systems usually offer the alcoholic criminal the least expensive and consequently briefest therapy. To reject this utilitarian practice in favor of an individual rights standard offering longer and more intensive help will require written legal guarantees. On the other hand, without specific clauses stipulating length of therapy, officials could restrain in residential institutions persons whom they could not keep legally in prison for extended periods.

There was strong survey opposition — 79 percent — to threatening an alcoholic criminal with jail unless he agrees to take the drug Antabuse, although such a measure would fulfill the utilitarian purpose of keeping the alcoholic sober and attentive during counseling sessions without physically harming him. The right of a legally competent individual to refuse to swallow a drug is one that society values strongly.

Could this forceful view also require legal protection some time in the future? Dr. Branko Gacic, of the Institute for Mental Health, Center for Family Therapy for Alcoholism, in Belgrade, Yugoslavia, claims very high success rates, from 60 to 80 percent, in getting his patients permanently sober. "The trick," he says, "is to involve the whole family in therapy and require the drinker to take disulfiram during this period, maybe a year. In the U.S., the therapists and alcoholics, they don't like to pressure people to take drugs. But it works.

"The kinds of alcoholics who most need help, who are most resistant in our sessions, will of course most oppose taking a chemical they know will prevent them from drinking. So we say they must swallow disulfiram every three days. Our patients now accept it as if it were penicillin. They want it for their better health. And this change will happen I think in the U.S., too. Your judges will begin to require disulfiram."

Gayle Rosellini, who supervised a U.S. drunk driver program for seven years, also strongly favors laws that can require Antabuse. She tells about Bill M., who said, "I would never have quit drinking if I hadn't been required to take monitored Antabuse and breath tests. I hated you for taking away my drinking. But now that I'm sober and in Alcoholics Anonymous, I know this program was the best thing that ever happened to me."

Sixty-two percent of those questioned were ready to support a procedure that conflicts with a present safeguard of American individual rights: applying compulsory therapy laws to alcoholics who have neither violated a law or are involved in family conflicts. An alcoholic, who, for example, is working poorly may be told by his boss to go for treatment or risk losing his job. Many such workers never enter or soon drop out of this therapy. The employer is just left with the choice of imposing penalties on the employee, including dismissal for unsatisfactory job performance.

In contrast, a Czechoslovak law reasons that it makes no sense to identify an alcoholic and then let him drink himself to death. If a Czech worker fails to complete treatment or cooperate with the therapists, the government can then order, under a threat of a fine or jail sentence, "compulsory clinical treatment." The drinker's only offense, as the law says, is "due to consuming alcoholic beverages repeatedly, [he] arrives in a state unfavorably influencing . . . his work performance."

If this law existed in the United States, it would complete coercion's net, encompassing driving offenses, criminal acts, family disputes, and now the daily job. As government worries about an ever more fragile U.S. economy, could America's values eventually accept this extension of coercion? How can the supporters of individual rights condition legislators to believe that compulsory treatment measures should exclude the alcoholic who only harms himself?

Bernd Schulte is an attorney with Munich's internationally known Max Planck Institute and its program to study international laws. The project has a strong bias toward protecting personal rights; for example, its report on public assistance in European nations criticized "the investigation of financial resources [because] it invades personal privacy" and other "interferences in the daily lives of recipients, e.g., cohabitation restrictions, rules that income earned from other jobs will be deducted."

Schulte and other German lawyers agree that there is a national bias toward protecting personal rights, arising from the Nazi heritage which left the nation very sensitive to laws that try to change individual behavior. Germany uses legal compulsion only to get treatment for alcoholics who are criminals and minors. In addition, German therapists have not been as exposed as their U.S. counterparts to the successes of intervention through job and family confrontations. "But as the German public and professionals become more aware of alcoholism's damages," says Schulte, "and that coercion can work to get more alcoholics into treatment, the country's resistance to court pressures will decrease."

Finally, 39 percent of the respondents to the international

poll questioned the law that pressures the alcoholic on public assistance into help. A diabetic on welfare who is unable to work because he fails to adhere to a restricted diet and take medicine is not forced to go for therapy. Laws that single out certain groups of citizens erode the ethical basis of a legal system.

Morris R. Cohen, a leading legal philosopher in the early 1900s, wrote: "That legal justice in some way demands the principle of equality seems certain. But what exactly do we mean by equality before the law? In the end nothing more than fidelity to the classification that the law has already laid down."

Fidelity to a classification system that attaches different values to the same behavior, depending on who is practicing it, is dangerous. Certain groups of people then have their choices limited, their autonomy interfered with, and a stigma placed on them, while others who have committed the same act do not.

Ethical Laws

What clauses could be written into the new coercive measures to satisfy an ethical standard that gives priority to the rights of individuals? Such safeguards rarely exist at present.

One obvious provision would specify that the alcoholic has the right of a court review. U.S. law allows a person denied a driver's license or welfare to appeal to the courts, but persons intimidated by coercion's threats and suffering from alcohol's instability may not be aware of this right. Unruly, drunk clients may not be told of this opportunity by the welfare or motor vehicle department employees. The alcoholic may seek advice at a neighborhood center, but the social workers there may be ignorant of the legal right of judicial appeal. (The international survey, half of whose respondents were government officials, was split on this question, with a small majority, 56 percent, in favor of the alcoholic having the specific right to either an initial court hearing or subsequent court appeal.)

Florida's 1977 Myers Act, which allows courts to commit chronic street drunks to residential facilities for therapy, specifies: "The person . . . shall be informed of his right to contest the application, to be represented by counsel at every stage . . . and to have counsel provided for him by the court if he wants the assistance of counsel and is financially unable to obtain counsel."

Court review is no guarantee, however, that individual rights will be protected. New York State previously had an involuntary commitment procedure for alcoholics whose thinking was so confused that they were in danger of harming themselves. After two psychiatrists had confirmed that this danger existed, there was a court review. Dr. Sheila Blume, medical director of the National Council on Alcoholism and formerly director of a treatment clinic on Long Island, noted, "Once a lawyer was able to get his wife committed to us so he could get her property. She wasn't alcoholic."

A second protection concerns the alcoholic, like Joel, who claims "irreparable" injury if pressured to accept treatment now. Regulations could give a judge the power to delay the legal threat and instead order an adjournment so the alcoholic could go voluntarily to therapy.

The presumption would be that alcoholics, suffering from the "disease of denial," will routinely try to argue for these delays. An individual could prove he recently saw a doctor about his drinking, intended to get help on his own at a certain clinic, and would suffer an unnecessary stigma in the neighborhood or at work if compelled to go to a clinic immediately.

Hungarian law, for example, notes that: "Alcoholics can submit, during the procedure imposing compulsory care and treatment, a request to undergo voluntary care and treatment. However, if deliberate behavior by the alcoholic results in such care and treatment being unsuccessful, the competent health authority is to impose a compulsory procedure, and no further requests for voluntary care and treatment may be considered."

Coercion laws tend to focus on the stable, working alcoholic.

Transient, skid-row alcoholics, those the public sees as "revolving door" drunks, are rarely offered the treatment alternative when coming to welfare's attention (they just stay on the rolls) or committing a criminal offense (they go to jail). This denies them the right to get help given other alcoholics.

L. R. H. Drew, a senior advisor on alcohol and drug dependence with Australia's Department of Health, supports this utilitarian practice: "In Australia there is much concern about civil liberties. It would therefore appear paradoxical to recommend laws to deprive a person of their right to refuse treatment or freedom of movement on the basis of alcohol misuse particularly in view of the fact that the value of treatment is uncertain."

But some success through alcohol therapy has been achieved for these groups as is noted in the U.S. government's statistics reporting an 18 percent success rate for transients and Pioneer Center North's finding that 20 percent of its patients had remained sober for fifteen months after discharge. Recognizing that recovered alcoholics often have a history marked by "slips" or unsuccessful treatment attempts, coercion laws could specify that the choice of therapy must be offered equally to all alcoholics regardless of their treatment histories.

The following case explains why such a provision is needed. It is from the *Lakeville Journal*, which reports on events in the picturesque farming area of northwest Connecticut:

> A Salisbury man was sentenced Wednesday in Salisbury Superior Court to four years imprisonment for third-degree burglary.
>
> A few observers gasped as Judge T. Clark Hull imposed the sentence on Richard Morey, 25. Hull cited Morey's lengthy record and the need to protect society as justification for the stiff sentence.
>
> Morey was convicted of robbing the Salisbury Package Store of $200 and several bottles of liquor on the night of April 12. In pleading Morey's case, Public Defender Stanley Herman said that he is a law-abiding citizen while sober.

Unfortunately, Herman said, Morey is an alcoholic and efforts to stop his drinking have failed. Herman said all of his criminal activity was committed while drunk.

Florida's Myers Act meets this need by declaring: "No person shall be denied treatment solely because he has withdrawn from an inpatient or outpatient facility against medical advice on one or more prior occasions, or because he has relapsed one or more times after earlier treatment."

Equality becomes an issue for all alcoholics when intervention procedures single them out unfairly. Why is the alcoholic on welfare required to get treatment but not the diabetic who is unemployed because he refuses to follow a proper diet and take his medication?

Lawmakers could write in such legislation a clause requiring all similarly ill persons who are without work to get therapy. If later shown that the law is being only applied to alcoholics, it can be struck down in court as violating the Constitution's requirement of "equal protection of the laws" (Fourteenth Amendment).

The length of treatment also should be specified to prevent government or courts from using a coercive therapy law to confine a person. The alcoholic, for example, might accept lengthy therapy in order to avoid even the short-term horrors of jail or to avoid the stigma of having "served time." Compulsory legislation could specify that the length of therapy cannot exceed either the alternative prison term or a specific period — perhaps one year — for welfare, drunk driving, family court, and other nonprison offenses. If longer treatment is required, the clinic medical director can petition for an extension, with the alcoholic having an opportunity to oppose this request.

On the other hand, treatment workers should challenge those statutes that allow loose bureaucratic practices which defeat the intent of coercion. A good example is New York

State's policy of restoring the alcoholic driver's suspended license regardless of whether treatment was completed. A coercive procedure bill should state that the mandated treatment must be completed and of sufficient length to have a reasonable chance of creating abstinence.

The kind of treatment offered also presents an ethical question. Most often alcoholics are sent for outpatient visits, about one hour each week for about fifteen sessions over a ten-month period. In New York City, the Medicaid cost for this therapy is $60 a visit or about $900, which is a higher amount than allowed in some states. Studies on legal coercion, however, reveal better success rates with more intensive inpatient therapy; up to 50 percent of court-ordered patients became sober through month-long, residential treatment at Minnesota's Hazelden Clinic. This therapy also costs more, at least $100 a day or a total of $3,000.

Residential treatment places a large financial burden on public and private insurance. However, if outpatient therapy is of little help to certain angry, confused alcoholics, neither the alcoholic nor public gains, and the insurers will continue to pay for the person's alcohol-caused health problems.

In 1967 the World Health Organization issued a report emphasizing that there was no one way to treat alcoholics and that appropriate therapy depended on the individual's drinking pattern and psychological, social, and economic circumstances. Members of a WHO committee on alcohol legislation meeting in 1982 agreed that this recommendation for varied treatment choices is often overlooked because of time pressures and limited government finances. Coercion laws could require that the judge or administrator indicate in his decision that the treatment ordered for the particular alcoholic be the one most likely to achieve sobriety.

Through specific protections supporting individual rights, the compulsory procedure laws should influence legislators to reject proposals that give states the power, such as Oregon now has, to require an alcoholic offender to take Antabuse. Forcing someone to take a drug violates Kant's basic definition of "Right." It not only interferes with a present "act of will" but also, for a time, future free acts of will.

In addition, some individuals have a constitutional right to refuse Antabuse for religious or medical reasons. All alcoholics, therefore, cannot be treated equally with respect to this drug. A law that places harsher obligations on certain people fails the basic ethical test of equality.

Religions and physical disqualifiers do exist of course for the military draft. Since World War I the need to defend the nation has been sustained as constitutional under utilitarian reasoning: selective service is necessary to the public. Without such a life-and-death link to the nation's well-being, the alcoholism treatment requirements should have to satisfy the more rigorous individual rights standard, which rejects a law such as one mandating Antabuse that cannot affect all people equally.

The public must be ready to pay for its values, however. Some Oregon alcoholics (though an unknown number) do stay sober only because they have been legally ordered to take disulfiram. (A treatment clinic can, as a medical decision, require an alcoholic to take Antabuse. If the patient refuses, he has to find a facility that does not impose this requirement.)

By consistently defining laws through an individual rights stance, legislators will know and understand why they should not consider a law like Czechoslovakia's that makes alcoholism therapy compulsory for a person who harms no one but himself.

Kant said, "Right, therefore, comprehends the whole of the conditions under which the voluntary actions of any one Person can be harmonized in relation with the voluntary actions of every other Person." Since an employer always has the right to fire an alcoholic if he refuses treatment, his relationship with the alcoholic is always capable of being "harmonized." There is no need for government intervention.

This means an alcoholic employee who refuses therapy will

likely lose his or her job and may go on to drink himself or herself into skid row or a hospital bed or a voluntary awareness that he or she needs treatment. But, again, a society based on individual rights at times will have to pay to protect this value.

An alcoholic who worked as a shipping clerk in a college warehouse was recently told to go for outpatient treatment at a hospital. The sympathetic supervisor had learned about the man's problem from his desperate, crying wife. The worker's hospital bill would be paid by his employee insurance and he would not lose any job rights unless he did not go for treatment. The man refused, arguing that all his job performance reviews were positive. When the college persisted, the worker hired a lawyer who filed a complaint with the New York State Human Rights Commission. The Commission upheld the complaint, noting that as long as an employee worked well he had a right to be alcoholic.

The Past

"When we invade, whatever our justification, another's sphere of rights, something very much like feelings of guilt . . . are understandable and appropriate," comments Professor Herbert Morris, professor of law and philosophy at the University of California in Los Angeles. He refers to the dilemma of people whose values emphasize personal freedom but who also recognize the need for a legal procedure like coercive therapy for alcoholics.

Uneasiness about government intervention also arises from examples of how easily laws that attempt to correct people's lives can feed on themselves and become destructive. The Nazi era offers the most recent reminder.

An international committee studying the notorious concentration camp of Dachau compiled a fascinating record of how a dramatically changed government and devastated economy soon warped coercive therapy laws by interpreting them through a sick utilitarian vision.

One of the Nazis' first acts in Bavaria was to declare attempted suicide a crime. The state needed the right to intervene in the life of someone who was harming himself and so also his ability to support the general welfare. "Persons who commit suicide harm state interest, i.e., potential labor force, military service," stated the 1933 law of Bavaria.

In March 1937, a protective custody law was passed to remind Germans not "to deliberately ignore their duties to the community or endanger state security. They must submit themselves to the national interests and respect state discipline." Nonconforming, nonproductive behavior would be punished. The utilitarian approach was to teach offending individuals while also helping the state. As a result persons would receive therapy through the lesson of laboring to build the residential facilities where they would stay.

This thinking spread to police officers with the order of October 26, 1939. The regulation described a practical way to make sure protective custody worked well: "In order to reach an intimidating effect, in the future the following should be observed in each individual case . . . Under no circumstance is the duration of protective custody to be disclosed. All inquiries from the outside as to the duration of protective custody are to be answered with 'until further notice.' " Not knowing how long he would have to stay, the individual was expected to cooperate better with the prescribed therapy, "obedience-diligence-honesty-order-cleanliness-temperance-truth-sacrifice-and-love of one's country."

The most utilitarian way to protect society from a repetition of the harmful behaviors became clear with the cooperation of health officials. Dr. Julius Moffat, who was medical director at Dachau, would remember in his affidavit that, "In December 1941 the first trainload of several hundred prisoners selected by the psychiatrists' commission left for Mathausen concentration camp to be gassed."

On October 4, 1943, Heinrich Himmler commented on how the personal character of those involved with directing coercive procedures had improved by "having endured this experience (the gas chambers) without losing our decency apart from occasional signs of human weakness. It has hardened us. This is a glorious page of our history."

As Dr. Veronique Bähler, director of an alcoholism program in Geneva, noted, "Of course, laws will help us get more alcoholics into treatment. In this sense, save lives. But musn't there be limits?"

After reading one of my magazine articles about the potential of coercive treatment laws to help alcoholics, the director of a well-known New Jersey alcoholism program wrote an emotional note in support of such legislation: "It's so good, relevant. I don't think coercive treatment should be discredited because some nonalcoholics get caught in the net, and I also think that tons can be done to stroke people into treatment as the more attractive of alternatives . . . But the civil liberties people who have argued against us withholding public assistance to sick alcoholics unless they receive some sort of treatment give me a strict pain — in the usual quarters."

Her letter helped me realize how even people dedicated to helping the alcoholic can be overwhelmed by a potential breakthrough in their uphill struggle and so forget the rights that alcoholics as individuals must maintain — for their own benefit and society's.

An official with South Africa's Department of Health, Welfare and Pensions complained to me about "all the emphasis on human rights. They worry so much about having too tough laws, so what happens? Many alcoholics who could be helped are allowed to just keep drinking."

His remark came during a discussion of South Africa's legal procedure that can require the court-referred alcoholic who has completed five to seven months of residential treatment to see regularly a social worker for up to three years. Follow-up counseling for an alcoholic who returns to life's daily stresses is considered crucial to treatment. In the United States it is often neglected as alcoholics drift away from their clinics. Because of its after-treatment mandate, South Africa can claim a higher success rate than any other nation attributes to its legally coerced patients.

Eventually U.S. legislators will have to decide whether or not to adopt such long-term follow-up care into their requirements for alcoholism treatment. Will officials base their decision on the rights of individuals? For example, the right to be presented fair legal choices means that the treatment burden should not be out of proportion to the length of the alternative jail sentence or type of social wrong.

"The 'right to treatment' has been identified as a social obligation recently and only in the most advanced societies," wrote Giuseppe di Gennaro, an Italian health official, in a report to the World Health Organization. It would be a shame to allow laws adopted to advance this right to erode other individual rights.

The Future

The ethical standard set by Americans for the coercion measures should also shape the other government interventions that may attack alcohol abuse.

There has been an abrupt reversal, for example, in the legal drinking age set by states. The permissible age had fallen to eighteen, but in the last two years many states have raised this level to nineteen, twenty, or twenty-one, and the President's Commission on Drunk Driving recently called for a national standard of twenty-one. Sparking this change has been the growing awareness that alcohol abuse is responsible for half of all auto deaths. Studies have shown that raising the drinking age to twenty or twenty-one can reduce alcohol-caused crashes by more than 25 percent among the age groups affected.

"I understand the statistical proof and so why the drinking age is being raised, but I am still opposed," says Robin Room, of the University of California at Berkeley's Alcohol Research Group. "I think in the long run people, youth, develop best when they have rights given to them with proper education — not rights taken away. This I'm afraid is being forgotten or not being debated publicly."

Removing privileges can lead to inequality, since certain groups may find ways to enjoy their former rights. Middle-class youth, for example, can drive to states with lower drinking ages while their low-income counterparts without cars cannot.

Inequality can also result from higher alcohol taxes unless society has declared beforehand that its actions against alcohol abuse must have an ethical base. Such tax legislation could state, for example, that a specific part of the new tax revenues would have to be used for the problems of the poor, who are hurt most by stiffer sales taxes.

Karl Marx, in fact, thought the first communist revolution was going to start over an unfair law attempting to moderate alcohol consumption. Edmund Wilson writes in *To the Finland Station:*

> Later on — June, 1855 — a Sunday Trading Bill was passed which, in the interests of keeping the lower classes sober, deprived them of their Sunday beer; and the common people of London congregated every Sunday in Hyde Park to the number of from a quarter to half a million and insubordinately howled "Go to church!" at the holiday making toffs. Marx was ready to believe that it was the beginning of the English revolution and took himself so active a part in the demonstration that on one occasion he was nearly arrested and only escaped by entangling the policeman in one of his irresistible disputations. But the government gave the people back their beer, and nothing came of the agitation.

The ethical standard now established in the coercion laws also will affect alcoholism research. The future holds the possibility of identifying young children who are born with a physical predisposition to this addiction and then altering their body's chemical makeup. Government regulations might envelop these prealcoholic families. Most states already "have laws which result in compulsory neonatal screening" in order to identify certain hereditary diseases and treat them through diet and medicine, notes Ruth Faden of the Johns Hopkins

University School of Hygiene and Public Health. She argues against such routine in-hospital testing of the newborn unless parents consent to it and supports a Maryland law that states, "Before the administration of the test, the parent or guardian shall be informed fully of the reasons for the test and of his or her legal right to refuse to have the test performed on the child."

"Genetic screening and counseling are certain to become major components in both public health and individual medical care," concluded in early 1983 the President's Commission for the Study of Ethical Problems in Medicine and Biomedical and Behavioral Research. Headed by Morris B. Abram, the Commission urged discussion now on the "important ethical and legal concerns." Assuming the inherited "fault" for alcoholism is identified, how will society react? Will laws be adopted that require families with an alcoholism history to have their children tested for a genetic marker for alcoholism? Should society require the family of an identified at-risk child to attend drinking education programs after the child's birth? Should government also have the right to order these parents to give their children a drug to restore physical normality for alcohol? Violating families might not be able to send their children to school, in the same way students are now legally denied entrance until they are vaccinated against certain contagious diseases. Under threat of a fine or even jail, would identified at-risk youths, young adults, and adults be required to have their drinking habits monitored? If such a person becomes an alcohol abuser, should he be coerced into treatment if he refuses to go willingly, whether or not he has harmed anyone else?

The test for any major social movement is the impact it has on each citizen. U.S. society should decide soon on its standards for the expanding compulsory treatment laws. The tone has to be set now for the public policy and scientific thrusts of the near future that will target alcoholism and alcohol abuse, so they remain keyed to the rights of the individual, to the ethics of it all.

8

What Now?

This book has discussed the ways that Americans, through government policies, public education campaigns, laws, and research, can moderate their drinking, sharply reduce the occurrence of drunkenness-caused tragedies, and get millions of alcoholics into treatment. But will these changes happen? Or is this just one more book about a possible social breakthrough that will never be realized?

Politicians have traditionally avoided involvement with alcohol concerns, believing that these issues will not arouse voter enthusiasm and may possibly taint them in the public's eye — "he must have a hidden personal or family drinking problem," "he must be a rigid teetotaler who isn't like us." In addition, if the proposed initiatives to curb abusive drinking and alcoholism are introduced and fail, their political supporters will be subject to severe media and public criticism.

Reubin Askew, the former two-term governor of Florida, never drank because his father and brother had been alcoholic and he had seen alcohol's ravages. He was kidded in the press for this, remembers Frank X. Friedman, an attorney who worked in Askew's campaign, "and so Askew worried about having too much of a good guy image. There are a lot of people in Florida who are stiff drinkers, and that kind of image can create a backlash."

Robert Wagner, Jr., deputy mayor of New York, knows politicians well: his father was mayor and his grandfather served in the U.S. Senate. He also knows alcohol problems well as his mayoral responsibilities include supervising the city's municipal hospital system. Wagner says, "Alcohol-caused problems make up between 30 and 50 percent of admissions in our facilities, and for most of them it's close to 50 percent. Alcohol problems are by far our biggest and costliest concern. But we don't have political support to shift around existing funding to put more into preventing abusive drinking, rather than waiting to see its effects. Politicians like too many people tend to see alcohol difficulties as someone's personal worry. They don't want to get involved, take leadership in this area, and move us on the road of prevention. Politicians will have to feel pressure to change."

Your Drinking and the Nation's

How can readers who want to achieve healthy, moderate drinking pressure politicians to advance the proposals that would help limit American consumption? Government officials will rally behind a new lifestyle only after a noticeable number of people have adopted it. For then politicians feel secure in their actions.

A great many health-conscious individuals had to display certain new attitudes and behaviors before politicians would champion nonsmoking sections on airplanes, trains, and buses, pass laws that require special lanes on streets for joggers and bicyclers, and demand that foods list their ingredients. Similarly, a sizeable percentage of Americans will have to adopt moderate drinking limits for themselves before legislators will advance proposals that intervene in the way the nation drinks. This behavior change would become visible in homes, bars, and restaurants and at large social functions. Individuals might tell someone not to have another, in the same way people now feel comfortable talking to others, even strangers, about their smoking.

Probably the major concern of a health-conscious people is what goes into their bodies. First of all, that means food. The health-aware individual should think of alcohol consumption in the same way that he considers food intake and consciously limits himself in order to look, feel, and be healthier.

Most diet-conscious persons are not uncomfortable if others know they are deliberately eating less. The drinker needs to feel as comfortable as the moderate eater, who tells the host, "I'm sorry no more, I'm trying to watch myself," or simply, "No, thanks." He achieves this by recognizing that, like the aware eater, there are millions of others like him who need to reduce their alcohol consumption in order to avoid physical problems, accidents, and excess weight. He is not weak or different for having to be conscious of his drinking.

Since alcohol affects people differently, an individual needs to determine his own drinking limits. At what point is he no longer just pleasurably relaxed but instead feeling alcohol's intoxicating effects and losing his ability to control his drinking? "When the alcohol interferes with how you think, feel or act normally, you've stopped drinking moderately," suggests Brinkley Smithers, president of one of the largest foundations in the alcohol abuse field.

Some foods, especially those containing sugar, can help certain people relax. When feeling tension, they reach for food. In a daily life filled with stress, this person risks becoming dependent on eating: his body and mind need food as frequently as possible.

The person who is prone to heavy eating resembles the drinker who often exceeds his limit. The imbiber should follow the same technique that the excessive eater uses: make rules. "I now eat only at meal times." "I know how many calories I can have, so if I take a dessert at lunch, I can't have one at dinner." "I take small bites and chew slowly."

To set alcohol limits, the drinker can follow several guidelines.

First, think of alcohol as a complement to meals and socializing and drink only at these times. Do not drink when alone or after stressful events.

Second, know his or her limit. If it is a maximum of two drinks a day, for example, keep to it. Occasionally this amount will be exceeded; so drink less or nothing the next day. The fit person also knowingly eats too much at times, but announces:

"I'll have to pay for this tomorrow."

Third, sip drinks, don't gulp them. Moderate drinkers enjoy an alcoholic beverage for its taste and its relaxing effects. Quick drinking produces alcohol's euphoria-buzz-intoxication, so the drinker escapes himself, forgets his personal rules.

Fourth, remain aware of what alcohol does. Many Americans now limit their intake of fatty, sugared, and chemical-packed foods because they have learned about their negative health aspects. Most social drinkers have almost no idea of what alcohol can do to their bodies. "Numerous information gaps and substantial misinformation relating to alcohol use exist among the American public," the Treasury Department has declared. Heavy drinking has been linked to cancer in the oral cavity area, liver problems, poor nutrition, decreased sexual function in men, and unattractive skin tone. It makes persons withdraw and be less communicative. Each alcoholic glass, goblet, or can provides a nutritionless, fattening drink of from about 80 to 150 calories.

Eating excessively overwhelms the body's ability to burn off calories, and this can create many problems. Similarly, the body needs about an hour to metabolize each shot of whiskey, glass of wine, or bottle of beer. Continuous, excessive, and hasty drinking allows a powerful drug to build up in the body. "People are unaware of the effects rapid consumption can have on the body," emphasized the Treasury Department's report on alcohol health hazards.

A high alcohol level in the blood will hit the brain, exposing the drinker to dangerous and often fatal accidents in the home, at work, or while driving. Each drink adds .02 percent to the Blood Alcohol Concentration (BAC). In many states, a BAC of more than .05 percent means the drinking driver is legally impaired, above .10 percent, legally intoxicated. Just three drinks in an hour can make a drinker impaired; for example, reaction time falls 15 to 25 percent, visual acuity drops 32 percent, and recovery from headlight glare is seven to thirty-two seconds longer. The only way to reduce excessive blood alcohol levels is to wait for the body to break down the alcohol at the rate of .02 percent BAC per hour. Exercise, coffee, showers are of no help. Only time works (or perhaps a sober-up pill in the future).

Fifth, appreciate alcohol for its taste. Many people feel they are drinking only when they sense a high. As a result they consume quickly and heavily to achieve and maintain this state. With dealcoholized wines and beer, a drinker can continue to enjoy the taste of an alcoholic beverage after he has reached his daily limit.

Like many coffee drinkers' initial experiences with decaffeinated coffee, imbibers may not find alcohol-removed beverages appealing at first. But they should keep trying them. Based on my observations, most people come to enjoy this lighter and less fattening drink. They find they can drink for taste.

Sixth, set a value on intoxicated behavior. Many Americans have a negative view of obesity (for which physical abnormality is not the cause). A person's failure to moderate his appetite seems almost without style or class. Someone who wants to drink moderately might think of excessive drinking in the same disdainful way. (This attitude exempts alcoholics, who suffer from an addiction or illness.)

Readers unable to develop and follow moderate drinking techniques may have a compulsion for alcohol, in the same way certain persons are compulsive eaters. The cause of such a difficult-to-control need may be physical, a cultural conditioning that calls for frequent alcohol use in times of personal discomfort, or an emotional need for quick relief from stress. The reason(s) is not known. No fault is involved, the person just needs help.

This drinker should look in the phone book under Alcoholism for the local council of the National Council on Alcoholism and visit a counselor there. This does not mean she is an alcoholic, that her mind and/or body is addicted to alcohol. The counselor may explain, for example, that her present heavy consumption is reactive drinking in response to a major stressful event — death, divorce, illness, loss of job — rather than daily pressures. As the tension fades the drinking can decrease if the person recognizes and adopts healthy drinking limits. "The crisis of divorce or separation, rather than the status of being divorced, is responsible for the elevated rates of heavier and problem drinking for younger women," remarks the NIAAA.

To determine if the drinker is actually addicted to alcohol, the counselor will ask questions about alcoholism's warning signs: Do you experience blackouts, temporary amnesia? Do you gulp your drinks and hide alcohol in the house to make sure there is always a supply? Do you drink in the morning to get started? When not drinking, are you especially nervous, perhaps even noticing yourself sweat, your hands shake?

A person is diagnosed as alcoholic based not on how much she consumes but whether this drinking has created continuous problems for her, with her family, job, health, and the law. The counselor must make the alcoholic recognize how drinking is harming her life, something the alcoholic may deny since she depends on alcohol's anesthesia to get through each day.

If this alcoholic accepts therapy, as a million and a half other alcoholic Americans do each year, she will attend Alcoholics Anonymous meetings or go first to a medical facility for more intensive help and then usually to AA. In treatment, the alcoholic learns about her inability to drink and also her inner strength; why she should and can cope each day in the same way every other recovered alcoholic does, without any alcohol.

Here's a test any drinker can take. At the next social occasion, don't drink although everyone else may be drinking. Be as talkative as anyone else without even holding a drink. If you try it, do you feel a certain sense of self — a natural self, containing "no additives, preservatives, or artificial anything"?

Citizen Action

Once more Americans have accepted moderate drinking

limits, public officials will be forced to consider this changing public opinion. It will become clear to them that most Americans are serious enough to support politicians involved in this effort.

The 1982 Gallup survey found that more Americans wanted government action to curb alcohol abuse than supported similar efforts to reduce smoking or promote better diet and exercise. Sixty-eight percent believed it was "very important" to have a national educational campaign to encourage moderate/sensible drinking habits, 61 percent supported a stop-smoking campaign, and 54 percent favored a focus on diet and exercise.

A majority of those responding were ready to make this a political question: 62 percent wanted their political parties to include a campaign for moderate drinking in their platforms. Fifty-seven percent called for a similar plank on less smoking, and 52 percent one for better diet/exercise. Similarly, 59 percent of Americans said they would be "more likely to vote" for a candidate who supports a national drive for moderate drinking practices, compared to 53 and 48 percent respectively for politicians involved with smoking and proper eating-dieting.

Sixty-two percent of those questioned said a moderate drinking campaign should be funded by government (state or federal). This was greater than the number of respondents who favored government-funded efforts to eliminate smoking, 56 percent, or improve diet and exercise habits, 51 percent (see Appendix B).

One explanation for this stronger sentiment may stem from the realization that better diet and exercise, along with an awareness of high blood pressure and less smoking, have contributed to a decrease in the incidence of heart disease and that a decline in smoking is expected to reduce the cancer rate. Alcohol problems, however, are reaching into people's homes at an increasing rate.

A Gallup Youth Survey revealed that the percentage of youths thirteen to eighteen reporting that "liquor has been a cause of trouble in the family " increased from 18 to 22 percent between 1977 and 1982. Overall, "as many as one American in every three says a drinking-related problem has caused trouble in his or her family," comments George Gallup, Jr.

A recent Louis Harris poll found between 1973 and 1983 the number of Americans who knew someone who drank excessively grew from 60 to 68 percent; and 56 percent of Americans now say a heavy drinker is "close to me."

The public is confused about what responsible drinking actually means, besieged by ads that say drink more, unaware of drinking's health impacts, and fearful of alcohol-caused tragedies. Asked if he was surprised at the poll's finding that Americans strongly desire a national campaign on moderate drinking, George Gallup, Jr., said, "No, not when you consider all the surveys. The trend, I think, is quite clear. People are coming to realize that alcohol abuse is the number one health problem in our society."

Following release of the Gallup poll's findings on the potential for a national effort to stop excessive drinking, the *Daily News* wrote a strong editorial declaring that this "educational program (deserves) wholehearted support by every citizen who cares about the nation's future."

A survey of Californians taken in 1974 and again in 1980 by the Field Research Corporation and the Social Research Group of the University of California also reveals the potential for public support arising behind government acts to moderate alcohol consumption. Ranking their main worries, Californians included crime, inflation, energy, unemployment, welfare, and the use and sale of illegal drugs. Alcohol problems and other health concerns were not in the top group. However, when asked whether they believed alcohol had a causal link to these major worries — on which government activity *is* expected — people responded affirmatively.

The percentage of Californians who thought alcohol was connected to violent crime rose to 59 from 47 percent between 1974 and 1980. Similar increases were noted in the percentage of those who felt alcohol abuse resulted in traffic crashes and deaths, which grew to 86 from 82 percent, and those who felt it contributed to divorce and family troubles, which jumped to 61 from 53 percent. Two other headlined areas directly linked to regular over-consumption — unemployment and industrial productivity — received similar recognition: Between 1974 and 1980, alcohol abuse or alcoholism, in the eyes of Californians, rose as a "major factor" in company absenteeism to 43 from 39 percent, and as a cause of unemployment to 27 from 24 percent.

Tracy Cameron, of the Social Research Group, concluded from these and other statistics: "Overall, 54 percent of respondents agreed with the statement that there was a great deal that community leaders or government could do about alcohol problems. In comparison, only 25 percent agreed that drinking is a person's own business and no concern of the community . . . The responses to these statements, taken together, suggest that Californians view the government or the community as having a legitimate role in intervening in an individual's drinking problems."

Easily the most dramatic, recent example of popular sentiment for political action on alcohol problems expressing itself took place in 1980 in Poland with the emergence of Solidarity, the independent labor union. Before it was banned by the government in December 1981, Solidarity pressed its list of major social reforms. Prominent among them were those connected to alcohol abuse.

Jacek Morawski, an assistant professor at Warsaw's Psychoneurological Institute, wrote the following for an international newsletter: "Measures against alcoholism were one of the main topics of agreement concluded in November 1980 between a government commission and a delegation of health service representatives, members of Solidarity. The protocol of the agreement carries, among others, postulates to work out a new law on the sale of alcohol, development of alcoholism treatment facilities, limitation of alcohol accessibility, banning of the sale of low-quality fruit wines."

To moderate consumption, Solidarity specifically demanded

increased alcohol taxes and the elimination of cheap wines, and to provide help for more alcoholics the union called for doubling the number of treatment beds. The hard-pressed civilian government then in power approved these demands because the resulting actions could affect both alcohol abuse and other visible social ills. Jacek Moskalewicz, a Polish health worker, commented: "Alcohol became a political question and the governmental response (of cooperation) was not for the sake of solving (alcohol) problems but rather to show that it was going to do something in the fields of social problems."

Dr. K., editor of a well-known Polish health publication and a member of Solidarity, recently visited America and when talking with me mentioned another early demand of the union. In the name of better productivity, supervisors in big plants were to stop ignoring alcoholic workers and instead pressure them to get help. "Action on alcohol abuse was among the early major changes that we in Solidarity expected government to make, to create the new spirit."

The Alcohol Industry Opposition

In nations where government does not have monopoly control over alcohol sales, the private beverage industry represents a formidable obstacle to changes that affect a nation's consumption levels.

After an eighteen-nation seminar on alcohol problems was held in 1981 in Vienna, James Mosher of the United States wrote a summary which noted that France's wine-growing areas were strong supporters of President François Mitterrand during his election campaign, and in England the beer producers were big backers of Prime Minister Margaret Thatcher. Because of such connections, there will be "even less interest in alcohol prevention issues in these countries," Mosher stated.

U.S alcohol beverage producers are also ready to make

costly investments to maintain political influence. "What that wealthy industry, which spends about $1 billion a year just on advertising, can contribute to influence political campaigns, plus the fear of politicians being tainted with the Neo-Prohibition label, gives us in America a real obstacle to getting political action on answers to alcohol problems," says John R. DeLuca. He should know; he served as director of the National Institute on Alcohol Abuse and Alcoholism under President Jimmy Carter.

DeLuca notes, "If I hadn't offended the alcohol industry I could have been in that job forever." He did offend them, he says, and because of this was asked to resign when Ronald Reagan became president.

The Washington experiences of John DeLuca reveal that the alcohol business will oppose any legislative changes aimed at producing moderate drinking behavior. The industry will fight government efforts to noticeably limit consumption, which in turn would limit profits. This almost guarantees that the public sentiment in America toward creating moderate drinking habits, if it stays alive, will eventually be forced to express itself politically.

DeLuca had been director of New York State's alcohol abuse agency. With a background in public administration, he was considered a professional bureaucrat rather than someone with a social mission, and the alcohol manufacturers did not resist his appointment. Arriving in Washington, he found an angry atmosphere: the Senate had just passed a bill, backed by such diverse men as Jacob Javits of New York and Strom Thurmond of South Carolina, which required alcoholic beverages to carry a label warning that overconsumption of alcohol could be dangerous to a drinker's health.

"This issue was one I inherited. It wasn't one I would have chosen. I could see the political pitfalls coming. But when I saw the testimony, the clear danger, I had no choice but to try to alert the public."

The House did not pass a companion bill, but the pressure for a warning notice led to hearings conducted jointly by the

Departments of Treasury and Health and Human Services, which eventually focused on a label to alert pregnant women to the risk of fetal alcohol syndrome and other birth defects.

"The Senate's proposed general health warning that 'alcohol consumption may be dangerous to your health' resembled the Surgeon General's smoking notice on cigarette packs," says DeLuca. "But the smoking label's goal is to eliminate all cigarette use, while the alcohol warning is meant to educate people about many dangers. A general notice on bottles and cans wouldn't necessarily alert someone to the different problems of alcohol consumption — with other drugs, driving, various health problems, the fetal alcohol syndrome. So we decided that the label should be just about one concern, the fetal alcohol syndrome."

In the committee hearings, the testimony clearly linked alcohol use during pregnancy to birth problems, although the medical experts hired by the alcohol industry refused to accept this evidence, pointing out (in the same way that the cigarette industry still argues against smoking's link to lung cancer) that each drinker is different and so it is impossible to determine that a certain mother gave birth to a damaged child only because of her drinking. But the question that truly could not be answered was the amount of drinking that caused birth problems.

While most birth defects resulted from heavy consumption — six or more drinks daily — it became clear that even two drinks could be harmful. Such social drinking was not a danger that the average woman drinker recognized. About 10 percent of women who consume "as little as one to two ounces of absolute alcohol (two to four drinks) per day during the earliest part of pregnancy produce infants with recognizable alterations of growth and/or morphogenesis," concluded the Committee on Nutrition of the Mother and Preschool Child of the National Research Council. "Because a 'safe' level of alcohol intake for pregnant women has not been established, the prudent recommendation is to advise against alcohol intake during pregnancy."

Julius Richmond, when Surgeon General of the United States, issued an advisory stating that doctors should tell pregnant patients that the best protection was complete abstinence. Such a notice mailed to busy doctors was very different from the federal government adopting a regulation that required a label on every bottle and can sold. To the beverage manufacturers, however, information on every alcoholic container not only would lead to reduced consumption by expectant mothers, but, more importantly, would open the door for a variety of government regulations to control consumption. The public would be alerted constantly to alcohol's negative impacts, and so begin to ask about the other grave problems caused by overconsumption, learning more about drunk driving, death from heavy drinking combined with other sedative drugs, the contribution of alcohol abuse to cirrhosis of the liver, and cancer of the mouth, pharynx, larynx, esophagus, liver and lungs. The more the public thought about these links, the greater the chance for citizens to call on government to moderate the nation's drinking.

DeLuca saw the power of the alcohol industry lobbyists reflected in the final report of the warning label hearings. The paper did not state, as DeLuca originally assumed it had to, that, since the testimony clearly linked alcohol use at an unknown level during pregnancy to the fetal alcohol syndrome, labels were needed on bottles and cans to alert the pregnant woman. The alcohol lobbyists had done their work at Treasury and Health and Human Services (HHS). The final document refused to take a position on whether or not a label was necessary. Instead, the alcohol manufacturers agreed to conduct a public awareness campaign about the fetal alcohol syndrome, with the two federal agencies monitoring this voluntary effort.

"But when was the last time you saw an ad on drinking and birth defects during a major TV show?" DeLuca reflects bitterly. "The alcohol lobbyists — oh, they came in with the slickest information — leaflets, public service spots for television campaigns. But then they make sure not too much information gets out. Because to really get to all pregnant women, to really worry them, you'd have to worry the entire public about its drinking. The industry never intended to do that."

The industry's down-played message: an expectant mother faces many health problems from, for example, obesity, smoking, poor nutrition, excessive drinking, and she should consult her doctor about them.

DeLuca suggested that the alcohol industry set aside 1 percent of its advertising budget, or $100 million, for a TV campaign about alcohol and birth defects. "I was turned down by the industry, whose wine and beer components are some of TV's heaviest advertisers. They had the nerve to tell me, 'The public doesn't really believe TV commericals.' "

The Treasury Department controls the Bureau of Alcohol, Tobacco and Firearms. Interestingly, when elimination of the bureau was proposed, Deluca recalls, the alcohol industry was a strong opponent to this step. From the very start of the debate the Treasury Department was against a warning label to alert pregnant women.

On the other hand, at HHS "there was no disagreement about the relation of drinking to the fetal alcohol syndrome," says DeLuca. "The one obstacle — alongside the reluctance to engage in a political fight — was the question of whether a label was the right way to educate the public. Was it a contribution to too much government regulation of people's lives? Secretary (Patricia) Harris was aware of the great controversy and big fight that promoting a warning notice would create. She decided to oppose it 'for the present.' "

DeLuca was contacted by President Carter's Domestic Policy Staff. It was considering overriding the report and adopting a warning label.

"I didn't call them, I wasn't going to go over the head of Secretary Harris. They spoke to me. Except I found out that the alcohol lobbyists knew every time I was supposed to meet with council staff. They knew about every piece of information I had been told to get. About each memo I prepared. Their weight in the White House was as powerful as in the agencies."

The industry's influence plus the timing — Carter had just lost the election to Ronald Reagan — killed the warning label in the domestic council. Stuart Eizenstat, head of the group, realized that besides the bloody political battle that would arise from approval of the notice, such action would mean having the lame duck Carter Administration enact a major controversial regulation in its last days. Eizenstat believed that this was wrong.

One last strategy was tried: bringing supervision of the sale of alcoholic beverages under the Food and Drug Administration (FDA), which could not only research and monitor the ingredients in bottles and cans but also require notices on risks. "Alcohol is the only major consumed item in the nation that the FDA does not regulate," points out DeLuca. "It is also one of the most powerful drugs we have." DeLuca's call for FDA jurisdiction was also defeated.

"It was crazy to believe that the industry would agree to do the most effective advertising possible to alert pregnant women. That would create awareness about alcohol's dangers and lead to more government moves. Yet their lobbyists sold this compromise. That's power."

DeLuca adds that in addition to those representing alcohol manufacturers, the lobbyists for restaurants, hotels, and liquor stores also can be called on to oppose legislation that will reduce sales.

When the Gallup poll revealing the public would support a national moderate drinking campaign was released to the press and created major headlines, the alcohol beverage industry reacted angrily. "Forget the 6.5 percent drop in supplier deliveries during one year, 1982," wrote Joseph Matzner, publisher of *Beverage Retailer,* a major weekly trade publication. "What we are facing is much more vulnerable to day to day business. Newspapers across the country are giving more than usual exposure to a Gallup poll . . . "

Before elected and appointed officials can be expected to intervene actively, significant public sentiment must become visible. It will have to be strong enough to outweigh the powerful lobbying and campaign contributions of the opponents of government intervention to achieve moderate drinking.

The Catalyst?

"Our poll shows that the support for achieving moderate-sensible drinking habits in America has the potential to be meaningful politically," says Robert Bezilla, the Gallup organization vice president who supervised the 1982 study. "But to make this force come alive, you need a catalyst, the first issue. The question is which one."

The initial spark might be through groups of individuals bringing lawsuits. Persons have sued unsuccessfully both the state and federal governments to demand that alcoholic beverages carry a label indicating the dangers associated with consumption. These suits charge that alcohol is an inherently dangerous product, and as such the law requires manufacturers to alert consumers to its risks. The courts, therefore, can order that such information be carried on bottles and cans.

One recent suit was brought by a man, who had been a heavy drinker for twenty years, against Heublein, the manufacturer of best-selling Smirnoff Vodka and many other alcoholic beverages. He argued that Heublein should have placed information on its bottles warning him that overconsumption could alter his personality, create an addiction, make it dangerous for him to drive, and cause physical damage. The appeals court in Chicago ruled, as have other courts, that alcohol is not an inherently dangerous product which must carry a warning from the manufacturer. The decision noted:

> A seller is not required to warn with respect to products and ingredients which are only dangerous, or potentially so, when consumed in excessive quantity, over a long period of time, when the danger, or potentiality of danger, is generally

known and recognized . . . The dangers of alcoholic beverages are an example, as are also those foods containing such substances as saturated fats, which may over a period of time have a deleterious effect upon the human heart.

The article sold must be dangerous to an extent beyond that which would be contemplated by the ordinary consumer who purchases it, with the ordinary knowledge common in the community as to its characteristics. Good whiskey is not unreasonably dangerous merely because it will make some people drunk and is especially dangerous to alcoholics. . .

Reviewing the Chicago decision, the magazine *Occupational Health and Safety* concluded, "The case was dismissed, but the idea that liquor distillers may be liable for injury their products cause is not necessarily dead."

Health professionals have argued that the relation of alcohol to birth defects is not knowledge that the ordinary woman or her husband would have. Legal suits requesting a label warning that "consumption of alcohol during pregnancy can cause serious birth defects" could eventually be upheld by a court under the inherently dangerous product doctrine.

A court victory over such a warning label might prompt the public to express itself through letters, calls, and the ballot and thus urge politicians to take further steps to eliminate alcohol abuse. The famous 1955 Supreme Court decision of *Brown* v. *Board of Education,* for example, ruled that segregated schools were illegal. That legal victory brought out the desire for widespread change harbored in blacks, leading to demands for new government policies in such other areas as voting, jobs, and college admissions, eventually forcing the U.S. government to accept an ongoing responsibility to intervene to protect people from racial discrimination. Ongoing government responsibility for the level of the nation's drinking is what the supporters of a national moderate drinking effort want.

Legislative Change

The few congressional champions of new alcohol abuse laws

have been recovered alcoholics, such as former Senator Harold Hughes of Iowa, who retired, and Harrison Williams of New Jersey, who resigned after his conviction in the Abscam trials. A notable exception to this pattern of political leadership was Pierre Mendés-France, the Socialist prime minister of France from 1954 to 1955. Fighting alcoholism, he not only argued for reduced consumption by young people but also purposely drank milk at formal dinners. His fight resulted in international publicity, and anger from his own constituency in Eure, a province that produced apple brandy.

Recruitment attempts have started to enlist more politicians around the question of how America drinks. This effort has been led by prominent recovered alcoholics. John Tucker, until recently president of the Florida Publishing Company, a major newspaper chain in the state, said at a recent conference in Jacksonville that he had just met with the mayor's first deputy for an hour and a half. "We spent a half hour on the new coliseum and the Gator Bowl and an hour on what the city can do to fight alcohol abuse."

Not long ago Tucker went to an important legislator in Tallahassee to request $400,000 for a new alcoholism treatment facility for Jacksonville. "I got other community leaders with me, and we told him simply, 'We need to have the $400,000 if you want our support for reelection'."

Tucker said his small but growing political force recently has expanded to include nonalcoholic individuals. Next it will attempt to get a tax placed on alcoholic beverages to raise funds for prevention and treatment.

Such traditional citizen lobbying efforts need time to develop. A few private leaders speak out for government action. Finally one issue becomes politicized and the public has a chance to express itself.

"I didn't start out to make alcoholism my issue — but my opponents forced me to, always referring to my past drinking," says Harold Hughes. He became his state's and then the nation's political leader for new policies to fight alcohol problems; the 1970 legislation that established the National

Institute on Alcohol Abuse and Alcoholism is called the Hughes Act. "There's no doubt that my alcohol work brought me votes, in all my campaigns. I could see it in the tally, though I couldn't measure it exactly. It was a lot of silent votes. They're out there."

In a 1982 lecture, Carol Bellamy, the New York City Council president, announced that she believed the solutions for alcohol abuse and alcoholism would increasingly enter the political arena. Perhaps recent events influenced her thinking. In mid-September, Bellamy thought she would automatically become mayor in January 1983 since Ed Koch was expected to win the Democratic primary for governor and then the general election.

But Mario Cuomo, the lieutenant governor, upset Koch. Cuomo credited his victory to the traditional Democratic coalition of unions, blue-collar workers, and minorities and said that the votes of the physically disabled also had had a measurable impact.

The disabled were neglected by Koch, Cuomo had charged during the campaign. The physically handicapped and their families organized themselves and came out as a voting bloc for Cuomo, in the same way that supporters for regulations to reduce alcohol abuse could make themselves known at the polls.

There are 10 million alcoholics and 30 million family members and other relatives close to them. If 30 percent of these 40 million people vote, that is a sizeable force of 12 million people. The Gallup survey noted that 59 percent of all Americans, not just those with this special interest in alcohol, would tend to vote for candidates who support a national campaign on moderate drinking.

Carol Bellamy also mentioned that the staggering cost of alcohol abuse was another factor that could force politicians to respond to citizen calls for government action. Officials would be publicly embarrassed if the media showed they were not supporting cost-saving changes at a time when money was *the* issue for society.

Which Issue Will Be First?

Parents with alcoholism in their families have a special interest in supporting politicians who seek government funding for research on a blood test that might determine whether certain children are especially prone to this addiction. The work on this test and the sober-up pill will not be completed quickly. Also obtaining government support for scientific research would not excite large-scale public involvement behind the moderate drinking proposals.

There would be a big payoff to government and to alcoholics and their families if elected officials promoted coercive treatment procedures. Opinion polls, however, show that the public has a low interest in the alcoholic, seeing him as a person who is weak, as the other guy. Achieving moderate drinking is a health-aware nation's main concern.

The two major thrusts by government that can affect consumption involve higher alcohol taxes and a national awareness campaign. The 1982 Gallup survey indicated that many Americans (48 percent for wine, 49 percent for beer, and 54 percent for distilled liquor) favored doubling the federal tax on alcoholic beverages, but only about 30 percent believed that doubling the tax would alone reduce consumption very much or somewhat. Higher alcohol taxes, if enacted, probably would not produce that initial, visible effect on consumption needed to arouse more of the public and more politicians.

The experiences of Norway provide a glimpse at what might happen if the national awareness campaign was attempted. The Norwegian government issued a White Paper on Alcohol Policy, which called for a continuing national information campaign whose goal was "to reduce the consumption of alcohol in all consumer groups." The Norwegian Directorate of Alcohol and Drug Problems concluded that this effort should allow Norwegians to enjoy the positive, relaxing aspects of alcohol while explaining to them that heavy drinking not only disrupted alcohol's ease but also led to drunk driving as well as many health problems.

Ragnar Waahlberg, of the Directorate, wrote, "It transpires that Norwegians do most of their drinking on Saturdays, whether at home or at parties. An average party may go: 7:45 P.M., preparty drinks; 8:30 P.M., dinner with wine or beer, and then coffee and brandy; 11:00 P.M., final beer and cocktails, one to two beers or cocktails an hour."

Waahlberg said, since "the last few drinks are the easiest to do something about," it was decided to try to get Norwegians to eliminate the custom of having a number of final drinks to complete the evening. The government needed a way to fix the public's attention on this goal. "We had to get people to talk about it (the need to curb late evening drinking)," said Waahlberg. "Make it catch on. Make the newspapers write about it. Broadcast programs on the radio about it. Get celebrities to try it. Get the whole country to try it. On the same day at the same time."

The technique chosen: all Norwegian drinkers were asked to take part in what was called Norway's "biggest alcohol experiment" on Saturday, November 14, 1981. On that day, every person would be asked to stop drinking at 11 P.M. The purpose was to show people they could enjoy alcohol just as much if not more by drinking moderately and to use this media-attractive effort to make Norwegians realize drinking was a major health decision.

From February 1 through November 14, the government conducted an intensive awareness effort about the benefits of reduced drinking. Ads appeared in magazines and newspapers, slides were prepared for movie theaters, and posters were distributed in schools, grocery stores, restaurants, and retail liquor stores.

Some public criticism emerged, attacking the campaign as "Big Brother," or as ridiculous because it wouldn't work, or as ineffectual since it emphasized moderation rather than abstinence and chose a time that was too late to stop a day's alcohol abuse. But the nine-and-a-half-month project went forward and succeeded in affecting the nation. Questioned in December, 79 percent of all Norwegians indicated that they understood the purpose of the experiment. Seventy percent said they did not drink at all on November 14; 7 percent drank but stopped by 11 P.M.; 11 percent continued drinking throughout the day; and 12 percent could not remember what happened. The large degree of recognition of the purpose of the campaign and acceptance of the government's role in leading it has led the Norwegian government to conclude that it will continue its efforts to change the nation's pattern of consumption.

A government-led awareness project in America would be a far more complicated task. The United States has significantly more people — 220 million compared to Norway's 4 million. A ten-month publicity and pamphleting effort would require an incredible expenditure. Finally, and perhaps most importantly, a Norwegian government monopoly distributes alcoholic beverages and so can post campaign posters in its retail stores as well as pressure restaurants and bars to display these signs and offer alcohol-free drinks. (On November 14, bars and restaurants sold three special no-alcohol mixed drinks, designed by the government, called the Olsen Driver, Turbo Driver, and After Eleven.) In the United States, however, it would be difficult to get facilities that sell alcohol to voluntarily distribute literature against heavy drinking, and the alcohol beverage industry would surely attack such a costly government effort whose long-range effects were unknown.

No one knows to what extent drinking patterns may be permanently altered by a project whose main purpose is to create an awareness of drinking as a health issue. The American Cancer Society's famed Smokeout, which began in 1977, when all of America's smokers are asked not to light up for twenty-four hours, only records how many Americans did not smoke on that day and for a brief time afterward. In 1980, according to the Cancer Society, 16.5 million Americans tried to stop smoking on the target day, 5 million succeeded, and 2.2 million were at least not smoking ten days later.

If a give-up-alcohol day is ever tried in America, the project might focus on a no-alcohol-before-6:00 P.M. theme. This would eliminate drinking at work and the after-job "extras."

The realistic goal would not be to dramatically alter drinking patterns with one special day, but rather to make Americans more aware of their drinking.

Then what moderate-drinking issue, which would not involve any great outlay of money or lengthy effort by government and could soon have a measurable effect on drinking habits, can citizens back? The answer is the warning label for expectant mothers. Eliminating alcohol during pregnancy could immediately wipe out the fetal alcohol syndrome and other alcohol-related birth defects and also save the nation a considerable sum of money.

"Fetal alcohol syndrome — a specific cluster of severe and irreversible abnormalities — is conservatively estimated at 1,800 to 2,400 births a year," says Dr. Edward Brandt, assistant secretary for health in the Department of Health and Human Services. "The incidence of a broad range of other adverse alcohol-related outcomes is as much as twenty times as high, affecting an estimated 36,000 pregnancies each year — or one out of 100 live births. And all of it is completely preventable."

Recently, Congressman Gordon Humphrey, chairman of the House Alcoholism and Drug Abuse Subcommittee, surprised many observers during a hearing by saying that he may drop his opposition to a warning label for pregnant women. In the past Humphrey had adamantly argued against general warning labels on alcohol beverage containers, but now he reasoned: "It is a gratuitous insult to the American people to have a warning label on an alcoholic beverage container that alcohol can be harmful to the health. I think everybody knows that, just as everyone knows that cigarette smoking can be harmful to the health. But on the other hand . . . I find that there is a very low perception and awareness of the likely effects on unborn children of alcohol consumption by the mothers."

At this House subcommittee meeting, a spokesman for the American Medical Association repeated its 1979 support for a law that required a label which read, "Alcohol may be injurious to your health, and if consumed during pregnancy, to the health of unborn children."

Fighting this sentiment, Rex Davis, head of the beer, wine, and distilled spirits lobbying consortium, complained, "Warning label legislation would denigrate this successful, cooperative program [the industries' voluntary education efforts about the fetal alcohol syndrome]; it would wrongly signal to the public that education efforts are not needed; and it would contravene the extensive study that government agencies and experts have devoted to this issue."

Why would adopting a label have to halt the research on the fetal alcohol syndrome or the alcohol industries' public awareness efforts to prevent abuse of their product generally? Humphrey asked. "If you are willing to have a public education campaign, why is that any different than putting a simple label on a bottle?"

Davis, of the Licensed Beverage Information Council, will have the industries' heavy funding available to fight such thinking by politicians. He will also have the industries' connections: Davis is a former director of the Bureau of Alcohol, Tobacco and Firearms.

Dr. Morris Chafetz, former head of the NIAAA under President Nixon and who now frequently speaks for the positions of the alcohol industry, has argued against warning labels. "They cannot deter an alcoholic mother from drinking, and the nonalcoholic mother does not need them." But no studies have been done on whether the special feeling an expectant mother has for her baby might be enough when aroused to stop her alcoholism, or get her to call for help, and studies do show nonalcoholic women are generally unaware of the fetal alcohol syndrome risk to them. Seventy to 80 percent of pregnant women in Canada drink despite present information efforts there and are at risk to alcohol-related birth defects, according to a report by Patricia Kelly at the recent Ontario Hospital conference.

The issue of drinking by expectant mothers also allows local government action, where it is easiest for citizens to become involved politically. New York City and State, for example, recently saw bills introduced in their legislatures, prompted by concerned individuals, to require retail sellers of alcoholic beverages to have warning posters in their stores that say, "Consumption of alcohol during pregnancy can cause birth defects."

More Than Alcohol

If a sizable number of Americans begin to support government measures to affect the nation's level of alcohol consumption as well as alcoholism, they could be the seed force for other social changes.

Americans concerned about protecting both themselves and the drunk driver also have to consider such possible government safety requirements as a system that makes a driver push a series of buttons in code in order to start the ignition, air bags, safety belts, a padded rear view mirror, and door reinforcements.

Alcoholics suffer from nutritional deficiencies. Besides affecting the body's ability to absorb certain vitamins, such as thiamine, riboflavin and niacin, alcohol fills up the drinker without providing nutritional value. In addition alcohol's disorientation creates haphazard eating habits. Nutritional weakness lowers the alcoholic's resistance to sickness and also his ability to work. A public, which wants to make compulsory treatment succeed, needs to limit the alcoholic's deterioration so he is best able to engage in therapy. This leads to trying to reduce the nation's consumption of additive and sugar-packed foods, perhaps by special taxes. Each American, for example, now drinks yearly a worthless forty gallons of soda, an average of thirteen ounces a day.

The Centers for Disease Control in its weekly report said recently, "Passive prevention measures, such as more widespread use of flame-retardant fabrics and smoke detectors, identification and reduction of fall hazards, sanctions directed at drunken boat drivers and prohibition of alcohol sale and use in recreational areas, should be implemented to protect everyone, including alcohol-impaired persons."

Since more than half of all Americans are already willing to pay a 100 percent increase in the federal taxes on alcoholic beverages to help moderate consumption, as public feeling around alcohol issues becomes more visible, the high tax proposal should gain sponsors among politicians. This cannot help but lead to calls for government to tax all luxuries more severely, placing more of the nation's tax burden on the wealthy. Luxury spending is "by definition the spending we can more easily forego," John Kenneth Galbraith has argued. Government's failure to place its taxing priority on these items, he writes, results "from fear of establishment disdain." The alcohol beverage industry qualifies as the establishment. Acceptance of taxes steep enough to reduce consumption and these companies' profits would spark groups arguing for high luxury taxes.

The low-income alcoholic's recovery rate can be 300 percent less than that enjoyed by the alcoholic with a good job. Without regular work, good housing, and a way to escape the constant problems waiting on the corner, the poor recovered alcoholic leaves treatment to return to a life of stress, which originally pressured him to reach for alcohol's escape. Advocates of efforts for successful coercive treatment of alcoholics through the welfare systems and the courts cannot overlook poverty's problems.

Dan Beauchamp, of the University of North Carolina School of Public Health, believes many people will begin to support the solutions to reduce alcohol's problems, solutions which are necessarily intertwined as part of the "post-modern" movement. "I have in mind the ecology movement, the campaigns for consumer protection and product safety, the anti-nuclear movement, the emergence of a limits-to-medicine debate, and a broad concern with the quality of life and egalitarian values . . . These groups see uncontrolled technology, intensive consumption and the 'profits before safety' viewpoint as central characteristics of modern American society and a problem for the health and welfare of the public. . ."

Talking to citizens and health workers concerned about alcohol problems, Carol Bellamy said she thought they could have real political impact only when they had the backing of other groups. "If you want third-party reimbursement for nonhospital based treatment, for example, join with the New York City Business Group on Health or lobby the Chamber of Commerce and other business trade associations and enlist their support by pointing out the cost savings involved."

Bellamy, forty-one, concluded, "You must learn to be a political force at the polls. Analysis and coalition building for substantial reform won't be effective if friends of alcoholic treatment programs lose their bid for public office and unsympathetic candidates are selected instead. In the final analysis, it's as simple as that. As you join with other politically involved women and men, raise money for campaigns, enlist volunteers for electioneering, and demonstrate the ability to get reformed alcoholics and their families to the polls, you will gain political clout."

The fight against alcohol abuse has joined with other causes to fuel social change in the past. The Progressive campaign of 1912, for example, was an attempt to reform U.S. society through far greater regulation of big business and an assault on social ills. Led by Theodore Roosevelt, the party, though losing the election to the Democrats and Woodrow Wilson, received 4 million popular votes, outpolling the Republican party and its standard bearer, William Howard Taft.

Alcohol problems, dramatized through the calls for prohibition, were among the reformists' chief targets. "In time, the movement was to encompass prohibitionists, advocates of women's rights, businessmen angry over competition from the trusts," wrote Ernest May in a study of this populist force in American history. "Progressivism united many different impulses, but in broad terms it was a movement to remake America in a homogeneous, classless and virtuous image."

Leon Stevenson is a retired Navy commander, a decorated Navy flyer who knows well the rigidity of government at many levels. He not only was a career officer but also experienced the political scene when he helped direct the Navy's alcohol and drug program in Washington, D.C. Stevenson also knows the other side of the alcohol abuse picture, having retired to become director of a new inpatient alcoholism treatment clinic in Florida.

Says Stevenson, a tall, lean man, who talks deliberately, "The U.S. only reacts when it sees a crisis. But the businessmen around here, the recovered ones but now also the nonrecovered, they're finally starting to come out. They talk with the politicians. And that's how something starts. The politicians, they're learning what's happening, how much they can do. The crisis — it's always been here. But now it's being seen and felt. The move for real change — well, it's being started. By the people."

Appendices
Bibliography
Index
Acknowledgments

Appendix A
Excerpts from Coercive Treatment Regulations and International Opinion Survey

For readers interested in how governments actually word their coercive treatment procedures, the following are excerpts from some of the laws mentioned in chapter 5.

Canada

The 1981 amendment to Chapter 23 of the Mental Health Act of Prince Edward Island, which has been passed by the legislature but not yet signed by the premier.

Section 13: A police constable may enter private premises to remove a person considered by him to be suffering from mental disorder caused by the use of alcohol or other chemical substance and may use such reasonable force as is necessary to take a person referred to in those sections to an appropriate place . . .

A police constable . . . shall remain at the facility and retain custody of the person so taken until the facility accepts custody of the person.

Czechoslovakia

Methodological Directives of 17 February 1975.

. . . Type B treatment . . . also includes treatment ordered by the social welfare and public health divisions of the district people's councils, and preventive treatment ordered by a court, particularly in connection with a conditional sentence . . . Type B treatment normally lasts for four to eleven months and may also be given as the initial treatment in cases of slight oligophrenia (malnutrition), certain alcoholic psychoses, severe somatic complications due to alcoholism (cirrhosis of the liver), and alcoholism associated with other forms of drug dependence.

Type C treatment is intended for patients who have been ordered to receive institutional treatment or preventive treatment as for type B, including treatment in connection with an unconditional sentence (during which treatment could not be completed). Those patients who manifest a negative attitude to treatment are assigned to type C treatment. The period of commitment to the institution is at least six months.

In the course of institutional treatment, a patient may be transferred from one type of treatment to another, depending on his attitude to his condition and his cooperation in the treatment.

Hungary

Ordinance No. 3 of 3 June 1978 of the Minister of Health, amending Ordinance No. 15 of August 1972.

[Alcoholics can] submit, during the procedure imposing compulsory care and treatment, a request to undergo voluntary care and treatment. However, if deliberate behavior by the alcoholic results in such care and treatment being unsuccessful, the competent health authority is to impose a compulsory procedure, and no further requests for voluntary care and treatment may be considered . . .

The head of the detoxification department of a hospital establishment may request the competent health authority to consider compulsory institutional treatment whenever he has good reason to believe that treatment in a hospital establishment will be unsuccessful. Under the terms of subsection 3 of this section, the head of the detoxification department of a hospital may authorize the discharge of a person undergoing compulsory care and treatment if he considers that that person can be successfully treated on an outpatient basis at a clinic. In such cases, he must contact the clinic serving the patient's place of residence or work . . .

Persons undergoing compulsory care and treatment who change their address must notify the head of the consultation service, who must inform the health authority responsible for the new place of residence of the need for continued treatment. The files of persons undergoing care and treatment must be examined at the end of each year to determine whether care and treatment can be terminated; in that case, the persons in question are to be registered for purposes of aftercare.

Persons undergoing aftercare [are] to be examined at least once a year in order that persons no longer requiring aftercare may be removed from the register . . .

South Africa

Abuse of Dependence-Producing Substances and Rehabilitation Centres Act, No. 41 of 1971.

Section 29: Procedure for bringing persons eligible for admission to a rehabilitation centre, etc., before a magistrate: 1. Whenever there is lodged with or made before a public prosecutor a sworn declaration in writing by any person, including any social worker, alleging that any other person who is within the area of jurisdiction of the magistrate's court to which said prosecutor is attached, is a person who —

a. is dependent on alcoholic liquor or dependence-producing drugs and in consequence thereof squanders his means or injures his health or endangers the peace or in any other manner does harm to his own welfare or the welfare of his family; or

b. because of his own misconduct or default (which shall be taken to include squandering of his means by betting, gambling or otherwise) habitually fails to provide for his own support or for that of any dependent whom he is legally liable to maintain; or

c. habitually begs for money or goods or induces others to beg for money or goods on his behalf; or

d. has no sufficient honest means of livelihood; or

e. leads an idle, dissolute, or disorderly life, the clerk of the court shall, at the request of the public prosecutor, issue and deliver to a police officer a summons to be served on such person calling on him to appear before a magistrate within such area at a time and place stated therein, or if the public prosecutor does not request the issue of such a summons, a magistrate of the court in question may, on the application of the public prosecutor, issue a warrant directing that such person be arrested and as soon thereafter as practicable be brought before a magistrate within such area . . .

Section 30.6: If it appears to the magistrate, on consideration of the evidence and of any report submitted or furnished to him . . .

a. that the person concerned is such a person as is described in section 29.1; and

b. that he is a type of person who requires and would probably benefit by the treatment and training provided in a rehabilitation centre or registered rehabilitation centre; or

c. that it would be in his own interest or in the interest of his dependents, if any, or in the interest of the community, that he be detained in a rehabilitation centre or registered rehabilitation centre, he may, subject to the provisions of section 31, order that the person concerned be detained in a rehabilitation centre or registered rehabilitation centre designated by the Director.

7. The magistrate may, pending the removal of such person to a rehabilitation centre or registered rehabilitation centre, as the case may be, order that such person be detained in custody or released on bail as provided in section 32.1 . . .

United States
Delaware

Delaware Code, Title 10, Chapter 9, Section 921, the Family Court of the State of Delaware.
Actions and proceedings wherein:

a. A member of a family alleges that some other member of the family is by his conduct imperiling any family relationship and petitions the Court for appropriate relief.

b. The Division of Social Services or a licensed youth service agency alleges that the conduct of a child, or of his parents or custodians, or members of a family, imperils any family relationship or imperils the morals, health, maintenance or care of a child and petitions the Court for appropriate relief . . .

c. In such actions and proceedings the Court may make such adjudications and dispositions as appear appropriate.

New Jersey

Family Court Act signed into law in July 1982, which had been Assembly Bill No. 3747, an Act concerning juvenile proceedings and jurisdiction.
"Juvenile-family crisis" means behavior, conduct or a condition of a juvenile, parent or guardian or other family member which presents or results in (1) a serious threat to the well-being and physical safety of a juvenile, or (2) a serious conflict between a parent or guardian and a juvenile regarding rules of conduct which has been manifested by repeated disregard for lawful parental authority by a juvenile or misuse of lawful parental authority by a parent or guardian, or (3) unauthorized absence by a juvenile for more than twenty-four hours from his home, or (4) a pattern of repeated unauthorized absences from school by a juvenile . . .

[The court can] order the parents or guardian of the juvenile, or a family member contributing to the crisis, to engage in a rehabilitation plan of treatment services as ordered by the court under its authority to enforce litigants' rights, when the court has found that such person's omission or conduct has been a significant contributing factor towards the ineffective implementation of a court order previously entered in relation to the juvenile . . .

Oregon

Section 430.850 of the Mental Health Act: Program for Persons Convicted of Drinking Under Influence of Alcohol; Crimes Committed While Intoxicated.

Subject to the availability of funds therefor, the Mental Health Division may establish and administer a treatment program with courts, with the consent of the judge thereof, for any person convicted of driving under the influence of alcohol, or of any crime committed while the defendant was intoxicated when the judge has probable cause to believe the person is an alcoholic or problem drinker and would benefit from treatment . . . The program shall involve medical and mental treatment to include at least the supplying of disulfiram or any other agent that interferes with normal metabolic degradation of alcohol in the body resulting in an increase in acetaldehyde concentrate in the blood, at regular intervals and under close supervision and control.

TABLE 1. SURVEY ON COERCIVE LAWS*

	RESPONSES	
QUESTIONS	Yes	No
1. Should a person on welfare because of drinking be cut off from this support unless he goes for treatment?	61%	39%
2. An alcoholic is involved in a family court problem because		

Table 1. continued

	of his drinking. Should he be ordered to get treatment or risk a fine or jail sentence for contempt of court although he committed no crime?	50	50
3.	An alcoholic commits a crime. If given the choice of accepting treatment or going to prison, should such treatment be:		
	a. completely in lieu of a jail sentence, or	22.5	
	b. in addition to serving a prison term, or	50.0	
	c. up to the court's discretion?	22.5	
4.	A criminal offender chooses treatment. If medically necessary, can this obligation last longer than the alternative jail sentence?	93	7
5.	An alcoholic voluntarily goes for treatment but drops out prematurely.Should the court then have the right to tell such identified alcoholic to return to therapy or risk a penalty?	62	38
6.	If a court believes the success of coercive therapy will be improved significantly through taking disulfiram, should the judge require this alcoholic to take the drug?	21	79
7.	Can court-coerced patients be		

Table 1. continued

treated equally well as out-patients, living at home, instead of having to go for intensive residential therapy?	62	38
8. Should there always be a court review before an alcoholic is told to choose either treatment or a penalty? (A welfare center, for example, can now make this decision.)	56	44

*Thirty-six government officials and treatment center directors from sixteen nations answered this survey. The nations were: Austria, Belgium, Brazil, Canada, Egypt, Finland, France, Great Britain, Holland, Italy, New Zealand, Norway, Poland, Spain, West Germany, and the United States.

Appendix B
The Gallup Poll Results

Is the nation's new health awareness, which has had a dramatic impact on traditional eating habits and activities, capable of changing the nation's drinking pattern? That was the question I asked the Gallup organization. The resulting poll, based on a sample of 1,039 adults interviewed by telephone between July 9 and 23, 1982, revealed that Americans are more worried about their alcohol consumption than the way they smoke, eat, and exercise.

Most Americans will say that drinking problems are important but so are a long list of other public issues. The real test, according to the Gallup staff, was how drinking related to the other health concerns that had already affected the behavior of Americans. The first question asked if a national educational campaign was "very important" for "moderate/sensible drinking, reducing/quitting smoking, and proper diet and exercise." A campaign to develop moderate drinking practices was called very important by 68 percent of those polled; 61 percent rated a cigarette campaign as very important; and 54 percent considered a proper diet/exercise effort as very important (see Table A-1).

The sample was divided about equally on whether the federal government or private agencies should fund a national program on moderate consumption. Democrats were twice as likely as Republicans to place the leadership and financial obligation on the federal government (see Tables A-2 and A-3).

Politicians or groups concerned about shifts in public thinking will be interested to note that a majority, 59 percent, said it would tend to vote for a candidate who supports a campaign on teaching sensible drinking habits; 62 percent wanted political parties to adopt this effort as a party plank; and 71 percent said they would sign a petition demanding a national sensible drinking project. All of these percentages were higher than those produced when the same questions were asked about supporting politicians and political parties who would take positions on smoking or proper diet and exercise (see Table A-4).

Fifty-six percent of those interviewed favored doubling the tax on at least one type of alcoholic beverage, and 61 percent requested a federal law requiring calories and ingredients to be listed on bottles and cans of alcoholic drinks. Only about 30 percent of the higher tax advocates and 20 percent of the label supporters believed that such actions alone would reduce drinking either somewhat or very much (see Tables A-5 and A-6).

This sentiment for a national effort to help Americans drink sensibly/moderately should prove to be influential and long-lasting: people who are college educated and under thirty displayed the greatest willingness to support politicians and parties and become involved with activist causes concerned with alcohol consumption. Women and registered Democrats were more likely to support a national effort, although Republicans were the most likely to support a doubling of the alcohol excise tax (see Tables A-7, A-8, A-9, A-10, and A-11).

TABLE A-1. IMPORTANCE OF EDUCATIONAL CAMPAIGNS

The following question was asked of 1,039 respondents: "I am going to briefly describe three proposed national educational programs. For each one please tell me if you think it is very important, somewhat important, somewhat unimportant or very unimportant that we have such a program."

| | RESPONSE | |
| | Very Impor-tant | Some-what Impor-tant |
Program		
Encouraging moderate and sensible drinking habits	68%	22%
Reducing or eliminating cigarette smoking	61	24
Encouraging proper diet and exercise habits	54	31

TABLE A-2. WHO SHOULD FUND
A NATIONAL CAMPAIGN?

This question was asked of those who rated proposed educational campaigns for moderate drinking, smoking, or proper diet and exercise as very or somewhat important. (Some persons indicated more than one funding source.)

FUNDING SOURCE	Drinking (930 respondents)	Smoking (880 respondents)	Diet/Exercise (882 respondents)
Federal government	38%	37%	29%
State government	24	19	22
Voluntary agencies	34	39	45
Don't know	11	11	10

TABLE A-3. RECOMMENDED FUNDING
SOURCES BY POLITICAL PARTY

FUNDING SOURCE*	PARTY PREFERENCE		
	Democrat	Independent	Republican
For moderate/ sensible drinking program			
Federal government	46%	39%	23%
State government	26	24	25
Voluntary agencies	27	32	48
Don't know	10	11	10
For cigarette smoking program			
Federal government	48	35	23
State government	20	18	20
Voluntary agencies	31	40	53
Don't know	10	11	11
For diet/ exercise program			
Federal government	36	28	23
State government	25	20	21
Voluntary agencies	39	48	54
Don't know	9	9	10

*Some respondents suggested more than one source.

TABLE A-4. LEVEL OF SUPPORT
FOR EDUCATIONAL CAMPAIGNS

The 1,039 respondents were asked if they would vote for politicians who favored national educational campaigns on drinking, smoking, or diet and exercise as well as take other steps to support these efforts.

	CAMPAIGN		
ACTIVITIES RESPONDENTS WOULD PARTICIPATE IN	Drinking	Smoking	Diet/Exercise
Sign a petition	71%	67%	60%
Like to see parties support in their platforms	62	57	52
Vote for candidate who supports	59	53	48
Contribute to or join voluntary organization that works for	48	42	38
Join activist organization that works for	19	17	17

TABLE A-5. DOUBLING THE TAX
ON ALCOHOL AND TOBACCO

| | | DOUBLING TAX WOULD REDUCE CONSUMPTION | | | |
TAXABLE ITEM	Favor doubling tax	Very much	Some-what	Very little	Not at all
Distilled liquor	54%	7%	25%	35%	28%
Beer	49	7	24	34	31
Wine	48	7	25	35	30
Cigarettes	57	7	28	35	26
Cigars/pipe tobacco	54	8	26	35	26

TABLE A-6. CALORIE AND INGREDIENT LABEL

The following questions were asked: should there be a federal regulation requiring beverage containers to list calories and ingredients, and would this label reduce drinking in the U.S.

SUPPORT FOR AND BELIEVED EFFECT OF LABELING	PERCENTAGE OF RESPONDENTS
Federal labeling requirement	
Yes	61%
No	31
No opinion	8
Label would reduce consumption	
Very much	5%
Somewhat	16
Very little	36
Not at all	38
No opinion	5

TABLE A-7. SUPPORT FOR MODERATE
AND SENSIBLE DRINKING PROGRAMS
— BY RESPONDENT AGE

	RESPONDENT AGE		
SUPPORT FOR PROGRAM	Under 30 (310 respondents)	30–40 (386 respondents)	50 and over (334 respondents)
Rate program very important	64%	71%	67%
Commitment			
Sign petition	80	80	57
Like to see parties support in their platforms	72	65	53
Vote for candidate who supports	67	62	51
Join or contribute to voluntary organization	57	56	33
Very likely to join activist organization	22	20	17
Favor doubling the tax on alcohol	56	59	54
Favor ingredient and calorie labeling	66	61	58

TABLE A-8. SUPPORT FOR MODERATE AND SENSIBLE DRINKING PROGRAMS — BY RESPONDENT EDUCATION

LEVEL OF EDUCATION

SUPPORT FOR PROGRAM	College graduate (536 respondents)	High school graduate (356 respondents)	Non–high school graduate (144 respondents)
Rate program very important	65%	67%	73%
Commitment			
Sign petition	76	72	60
Like to see parties support in their platforms	61	62	65
Vote for candidate who supports	60	55	63
Join or contribute to voluntary organization	55	47	36
Very likely to join activist organization	22	17	17
Favor doubling the tax on alcohol	65	57	30
Favor ingredient and calorie labeling	59	62	65

TABLE A-9. SUPPORT FOR MODERATE
AND SENSIBLE DRINKING PROGRAMS
— BY RESPONDENT SEX

SUPPORT FOR PROGRAM	SEX	
	Male (509 respondents)	Female (530 respondents)
Rate program very important	62%	72%
Commitment		
Sign petition	70	72
Like to see parties support in their platforms	59	65
Vote for candidate who supports	55	62
Join or contribute to voluntary organization	47	48
Very likely to join activist organization	18	21
Favor doubling the tax on alcohol	53	59
Favor ingredient and calorie labeling	55	68

TABLE A-10. SUPPORT FOR MODERATE
AND SENSIBLE DRINKING PROGRAMS
— BY GEOGRAPHIC REGION

SUPPORT FOR PROGRAM	REGION			
	East (282 respondents)	South (294 respondents)	Midwest (286 respondents)	West (177 respondents)
Rate program very important	69%	69%	64%	69%
Commitment				
Sign petition	73	70	68	74
Like to see parties support in their platforms	64	65	57	65
Vote for candidate who supports	58	62	33	61
Join or contribute to voluntary organization	46	47	50	47
Very likely to join activist organization	18	20	20	20
Favor doubling the tax on alcohol	32	59	55˙	60
Favor ingredient and calorie labeling	65	59	61	59

TABLE A-11. SUPPORT FOR MODERATE
AND SENSIBLE DRINKING PROGRAMS
— BY PARTY PREFERENCE

	PARTY PREFERENCE		
SUPPORT FOR PROGRAM	Republican (279 respondents)	Democrat (366 respondents)	Independent (352 respondents)
Rate program very important	65%	71%	65%
Commitment			
Sign petition	76	74	67
Like to see parties support in their platforms	59	69	59
Vote for candidate who supports	59	65	53
Join or contribute to voluntary organization	49	49	48
Very likely to join activist organization	20	20	19
Favor doubling the tax on alcohol	61	59	52
Favor ingredient and calorie labeling	58	69	58

Bibliography

The source of quotes and statistics is cited in the text. The references below are listed under the name of these persons or organizations. If no citation appears below, the information was gathered in conversations or correspondence with the author. Unless another federal document is mentioned, U.S. statistics come from the National Institute on Alcohol Abuse and Alcoholism's two latest reports: *Alcohol and Health: Special Report to the U.S. Congress* (June 1978 and January 1981).

Books

Allen, Frederick Lewis. *The Big Change: America Transforms Itself, 1900 – 1950.* New York: Harper & Row, 1952.

Armyr, Gunno, et al. *Alcohol in the World of the '80s.* Stockholm: Sober Forlags AB (ANSVAR), 1982.

Beauchamp, Dan. *Beyond Alcoholism: Alcohol and Public Health Policy.* Philadelphia: Temple University Press, 1980.

Brecher, Edward. *Licit and Illicit Drugs.* Boston: Little, Brown, 1972.

Cohen, Morris, and Cohen, Felix. *Readings in Jurisprudence and Legal Philosophy.* Boston: Little, Brown, 1951.

Distel, Barbara, and Jakusch, Ruth. *Concentration Camp Dachau, 1933 – 1945.* Brussels: Comité International de Dachau, 1978.

Englemann, Larry. *Intemperance: The Lost War Against Liquor.* New York: Free Press, 1979.

Frankel, Gail, and Whitehead, Paul. *Drinking and Damage: Theoretical Advances and Implications for Treatment.* New Brunswick, N.J.: Rutgers Center of Alcohol Studies, 1981.

Grad, Frank. *Alcoholism and the Law.* Dobbs Ferry, New York: Oceana Publications, 1971.

Institute of Medicine of the National Academy of Science, Health and Behavior. *Frontiers of Research in Biobehavioral Sciences.* Washington, D.C.: National Academy Press, 1982.

Kittrie, Nicholas. *The Right to be Different: Deviance and Enforced Therapy.* Baltimore: Johns Hopkins University Press, 1972.

Mahaffrey, Maryann, and Hanks, John W., eds. *Practical Politics: Social Work and Political Responsibility.* Silver Spring, MD: National Association of Social Workers, 1982.

Majchrowicz, Edward, and Noble, Ernest. *Biochemistry and Pharmacology of Ethanol.* New York: Plenum, 1979.

May, Ernest. *The Progressive Era: The Life History of the United States, 1901 – 1917.* New York: Time-Life Books, 1964.

Menninger, Karl. *The Crime of Punishment.* New York: Viking Press, 1968.

Moore, Mark, ed. *Alcohol and Public Policy: Beyond the Shadow of Prohibition.* Washington, D.C.: National Academy Press, 1981.

Moser, Joy. *Prevention of Alcohol-Related Problems.* Toronto: World Health Organization and the Addiction Research Foundation, 1980.

National Institute on Alcohol Abuse and Alcoholism. *Alcohol and Health: Special Report to the U.S. Congress.* Rockville, MD: U.S. Department of Health and Human Services, June, 1978 and January, 1981.

Pittman, David. *Primary Prevention of Alcohol Abuse and Alcoholism: An Evaluation of the Control of Consumption Policy.* St. Louis: Social Science Institute, Washington University, 1980.

Reverby, Susan, and Rosner, David, eds. *Health Care in America: Essays in Social History.* Philadelphia: Temple University Press, 1979.

Szent-Györgyi, Albert. *The Crazy Age.* New York: Grosset & Dunlap, 1970.

U.S., Department of the Treasury and Department of Health and Human Services. *Health Hazards Associated with Alcohol and Methods to Inform the General Public of these Hazards.* Washington, D.C.: Department of the Treasury, 1980.

Articles and Pamphlets

"A.A. Guidelines, Cooperating with Court, A.S.A.P. and Similar Programs," Alcoholics Anonymous, August, 1974, pp. 1–6.

Alcohol Beverage Executives' Newsletter. "To Keep You Up to Date," no. 2199 (May 7, 1982), p. 6.

"Alcohol Trauma." *Emergency Medical Services* (American Trauma Society) 6, no. 1 (1982), cover–3.

Alcoholism. "Red Head: Mysterious Malady Strikes Oenophiles," May-June, 1982, p. 53.

The Alcoholism Report, 10, no. 20, August 16; 10, no. 21, August 31; and 10, no. 23, September 30, 1982.

Alkana, R. L. "Reversal of Ethanol Intoxication in Humans: An Assessment of the Efficacy of L-Dopa, Aminophylline, and Ephedrine." *Psychopharmacology* 55 (1977), 203–212.

American Cancer Society. "The Great American Smokeout, Promotion Guide," 1981.

Babayan, E. A. "On a Policy for Alcoholism Control." Unpublished paper, 1982.

Bellamy, Carol. "Strengthening the Political Commitment to the Prevention and Treatment of Alcoholism." Paper presented at the Harold Riegelman Public Policy Lecture of the New York City Affiliate of the National Council on Alcoholism, October 5, 1982.

Blane, Howard. "Alcohol, Public Education and Mass Media, An Overview." *Alcohol Health and Research World,* Fall, 1980, pp. 2–16.

Bottom Line. "Heading into the 1980s: Abstinence Gaining," 4, no. 2 (1981), 14–15.

Brewers Digest. "Summaries of Analyses," March, 1982, p. 48.

Cameron, Tracy. "Alcohol and Public Problems: Public Opinion in California, 1974–1980." Unpublished paper, February, 1981.

Centers for Disease Control. "Alcohol as a Risk Factor for Injuries." *Morbidity and Mortality Weekly Report,* February 11, 1983, p. 62.

Chafetz, Morris. "To Warn or not to Warn." *Medical Tribune,* January 12, 1983, p. 36.

Chin, Jane, et al. "Increased Cholesterol Content of Erthrocyte and Brain Membranes in Ethanol-Tolerant Mice." In *Biochimica et Biophysica Acta,* Holland: Elsevier, 1978, pp. 358–363.

Chin, Jane, and Goldstein, Dora. "Drug Tolerance in Membranes: A Spin Label Study of the Effects of Ethanol." *Science,* May 6, 1977, pp. 684–685.

Cisin, I. H. "From Morass to Discipline in One Grand Leap."

Journal of Studies on Alcohol, Supplement no. 8 (November, 1979), pp. 27–33.

DeLuca, John A. "Stop the Discrimination!" *Advertising Age,* March 29, 1982, p. M16.

Distilled Spirits Council of the United States (DISCUS). *Annual Statistical Review, 1980, Distilled Spirits Industry.* Washington, D.C.: DISCUS, 1981.

———. *DISCUS Fact Book, 1979.* Washington, D.C.: DISCUS, 1980.

———. *DISCUS Newsletter,* no. 396 (December, 1981).

Emrick, Chad. "Perspectives in Clinical Research: Relative Effectiveness of Alcohol Abuse Treatment." In *Alcoholism and Health,* Germantown, MD.: Aspen Systems Corp., 1979, pp. 71–84.

Epstein, Thomas. "A Sociological Examination of Intoxication and the Criminal Law." *Contemporary Drug Problems,* Fall, 1978, pp. 401–458.

Faden, Ruth, and Chwalow, Judith A. "A Survey to Evaluate Parental Consent as Public Policy for Neonatal Screening." *American Journal of Public Health,* December, 1982, pp. 1347–1352.

Fagan, Ronald, and Fagan, Nancy. "The Impact of Legal Coercion on the Treatment of Alcoholism." *Journal of Drug Issues,* Winter, 1982, p. 103.

Farber, Leslie. "Ours Is the Addicted Society." *New York Times Magazine,* December 11, 1966, pp. 43–119.

Ford, Betty. "Betty Ford Meets the Challenge of Recovery." *Alcoholism,* Sept.-Oct., 1982, pp. 19–23.

Galanter, Marc, M.D. "Sociobiology and Informal Social Controls of Drinking." *Journal of Studies on Alcohol* 42, no. 1 (1981), pp. 64–79.

Gallup Organization. "A Survey on National Attitudes Towards a Potential Education Campaign for Moderate and Sensible Drinking Habits," July, 1982.

Goerth, Charles. "Alcoholism: Establishing Liability." *Occupational Health and Safety,* September, 1982, pp. 23–24.

Goldstein, D. B. "Some Promising Fields of Inquiry in Biomedical Alcohol Research." *Journal of Studies on Alcohol,* Supplement no. 8 (November, 1979), p. 204.

Goodstadt, Michael. "Public Attitudes Toward Increasing the Price of Alcoholic Beverages." *Journal of Studies on Alcohol* 39, no. 9 (1978), pp. 1630–1632.

Gordis, Enoch, et al.. "Outcome of Alcoholism Treatment Among 5,578 Patients in an Urban Comprehensive Hospital-Based Program: Application of a Computerized Data System." *Alcoholism: Clinical and Experimental Research* 5, no. 4 (Fall, 1981), pp. 509–522.

Greene, J. Michael. "The Bar That Bans Alcohol." *Newsday,* August 1, 1982, p. 6.

Greizerstein, H. B. "Congener Contents of Alcoholic Beverages." *Journal of Studies on Alcohol* 42 (1981), pp. 1030–1037.

Hammond, Robert. "Moderate Alcohol Use Threat to Liquor Industry." *Alcoholism,* Jan.-Feb., 1983, p. 63.

Hingson, Ralph, et al. "Seeking Help for Drinking Problems — A Study in the Boston Metropolitan Area." *Journal of Studies on Alcohol* 43, no. 3 (1982), pp. 273–288.

Hinkle, Richard Paul. "White to Light to Alcohol-Free? Maybe." *Advertising Age,* March 29, 1982, pp. M37–M41.

International Digest of Health Legislation (Geneva) 33, no. 1 (1982), p. 34.

Israel, Y. "Researching the Biology of Alcoholism: One Way of Seeing It." *Journal of Studies on Alcohol,* Supplement no. 8 (November, 1979), pp. 182–203.

Johnson, L. A. "Use of Alcohol by Persons 65 Years and Over, Upper East Side of Manhattan." Springfield, Va., U.S. National Technical Information Service, 1974.

Jones, Kenneth, and Vischi, Thomas. "Impact of Alcohol, Drug Abuse and Mental Health Treatment on Medical Care Utilization: A Review of the Research Literature." *Medical Care,* December, 1979, pp. 1–81.

The Journal. Toronto: Addiction Research Foundation, April, May, and December, 1981.

Kavanaugh, Carolyn. "A Special Report: Antabuse, New Concerns." *Amethyst, Multnomah County Alcohol and Drug Scene* 3, no. 7 (September, 1979), pp. 1–9.

Kearney, Mark. "FAS Information Campaigns Should Go to the Public at Large." *The Journal,* February 1, 1983, p. 4.

Kingstone, E., and Kline, S. A. "Disulfiram Implants in the Treatment of Alcoholism." *International Pharmacopsychiat* 10 (1975), pp. 183–191.

Kittrie, Nicholas. "Forced Treatment — The Future for Alcoholism?" paper presented at New York City Affiliate, National Council on Alcoholism, June 8, 1981.

Kramer, Hilton. "Partisan Culture, Partisan Politics." *New York Times Book Review,* February 7, 1982, p. 1.

The Lakeville Journal. "Salisbury Man Sentenced to 4 Years for Burglary," May 27, 1982, p. A3.

Laundergan, J. Clark, et al. "Are Court Referrals Effective? Judicial Commitment for Clinical Dependency in Washington County, Minnesota." *Hazelden,* 1979, pp. 5–13.

Lecos, Chris. "More Cups Lifted Sans Caffeine." *FDA Consumer,* May, 1980, pp. 23–25.

Lipsig, Harry. "Host's Liability for Intoxicated Guests." *New York Law Journal,* December 29, 1981, p. 1.

Looney, M. A. "Alcohol Use Survey on Campus: Implications for Health Education." *Journal of the American College Health Association,* 25 (1976), pp. 109–112.

Luks, Allan. "Compulsory Treatment for Alcoholics." *America,* June 19, 1982, pp. 474–476.

———. "Dealcoholized Beverages: Changing the Way America Drinks." *The Futurist,* October, 1982, pp. 44–49.

———. "How to Prevent Child Abuse." *Lady's Circle,* September, 1980, pp. 42–73.

———. "How You Can Help the Alcoholic." *Chemical Engineering,* May 9, 1977, pp. 149–151.

———. "The Law and Alcoholism." *Alcohol Health and Research World,* Fall, 1977, pp. 13–16.

———, ed. *Legal Issues* (Lausanne), November, 1980, June and November, 1981, March, 1982.

———. "Needed: A Center to Evaluate Alcoholism Laws." *Chicago Sun-Times,* August 28, 1978, pp. 28.

———. "The Sober-Up Pill: A Possible Cure for Drunkenness." *The Futurist,* October, 1981, pp. 23–29.

MacLennan, Anne. "Oil Spilling into Addictions Field." *The Journal,* August 1, 1981, p. 10.

Malcolm, M. T., and Madden, J. S. "The Use of Disulfiram Implantation in Alcoholism." *British Journal of Psychiatry* 123 (1973), pp. 41–45.

Manning, Thomas. "Light Beer: Hardly." *Modern Brewery Age,* July, 1982, pp. MS60–MS90.

Marco, Corey, and Marco, Joni Michael. "Antabuse: Medication in Exchange for a Limited Freedom. Is it Legal?" *American Journal of Law and Medicine* 5, no. 4 (1980), pp. 295–330.

Marlatt, Alan, et al. "The Think-Drink Effect." *Psychology Today,* December, 1981, pp. 60–69.

Matzner, Joseph. "Between You and Me." *Beverage Retailer,* February 7, 1983.

McConnell, Harvey. "Care Gets Sickest Drinkers off Dole and Back to Work." *The Journal,* June 1, 1982, p. 2.

——— "The Search for New 'Highs' Goes On." *The Journal,* August 1, 1982, p. 16.

Milio, Nancy. "Progress in Primary Prevention: The Smoking-Health Issue." *American Journal of Public Health,* May, 1982, pp. 428–429.

Miller, Jerauld. Editorial. *Alcoholism,* July-August, 1982, p. 9.

Morawski, Jacek. "Poland Announces Independent Alcoholism Fight." *Legal Issues,* November, 1981, pp. 1–2.

Morehouse, Ellen. "Treating the Alcoholic on Public Assistance." *Social Casework* 59 (January, 1978), pp. 36–41.

Morris, Herbert. "The Status of Rights." *Ethics* 92 (October, 1981), pp. 40–51.

Mosher, James. "International Trends in Alcohol Consumption, Alcohol-Related Problems and Alcohol Control Policies." In *Alcohol In the World of the '80s.* Stockholm: Sober Forlags AB (ANSVAR), 1982.

National Institute on Alcohol Abuse and Alcoholism. *Facts About Alcohol and Alcoholism.* Rockville, Md.: U.S. Government Printing Office, 1980.

National Research Council, Committee on Nutrition of the Mother and Preschool Child. "Alternative Dietary Practices and Nutritional Abuses in Pregnancy." Washington, D.C.: National Academy Press, 1982.

The Nation's Health. "Americans Lacking Nutrients," July, 1982, p. 7.

Newton, Jon. "Police Drug Powers Right for PEI says Addiction Services Director." *The Journal,* September 1, 1981, p. 7.

Paley, Marlene. "The Development of a Problem-Drinking Driver Program." *Alcohol Health and Research World,* Fall, 1981, pp. 55–57.

Payer, Lynn. "Jewish Culture Provides Impetus for Sobriety." *The*

Journal, February 1, 1982, p. 9.

Peltoniemi, Teuvo. "Alcohol and Family Violence." In *Papers of the 28th International Institute on the Prevention and Treatment of Alcoholism.* Lausanne: International Council on Alcohol and Addictions, 1982.

Perrin, Thomas. "When Parents are Alcoholics, Children are in Trouble." *The Record* (Bergen, New Jersey), March 1, 1983.

Phillips, Michael, and McAloon, Margaret. "Sweat-Patch Test for Alcohol Consumption." *Alcoholism: Clinical and Experimental Research* 4, no. 4 (October, 1980), pp. 391–395.

Prince Edward Island, Minister of Health. "Report of the Advisory Committee on Alcohol and Drug Addiction Treatment and Prevention Services on Prince Edward Island (and Dissent of Paddy Bruce)," October, 1979, pp. 1–115.

Problems Related to Alcohol Consumption, Report of a WHO Expert Committee. Geneva: World Health Organization, 1980.

Raspberry, William. "Distilled Wisdom." *Washington Post,* October 23, 1981, p. A28.

Richards, David. "Rights and Autonomy." *Ethics* 92 (October, 1981), pp. 3–20.

Rinella, Vincent. "Diversion Seen Less Likely for Alcoholic Offenders." *NIAAA Information and Feature Service,* September 29, 1981, p. 2.

Rosellini, Gayle. "Doing What's Indicated: DWI as Intervention." *Alcoholism,* July-Aug., 1982, pp. 31–33.

Sapontzis, S. F. "A Critique of Personhood." *Ethics* 91 (July, 1981), pp. 568–579.

Schmidt, Wolfgang, and Popham, Robert. *Alcohol Problems and Their Prevention.* Toronto: Addiction Research Foundation, 1978.

Schuckit, Marc. "Disulfiram and the Treatment of Alcoholic Men." *Advances in Alcoholism* 2, no. 4 (April, 1981), pp. 1–5

Schuster, Erich. "Konsumverhalten Und Alkoholgefährdung Bei Jugendlichen." In *Papers of the 28th International Institute on the Prevention and Treatment of Alcoholism.* Lausanne: International Council on Alcohol and Addictions, 1982.

Smith, Robert, M.D., et al. "Alcohol's Effect on Some Formal Aspects of Verbal Social Communication." *Archives of General Psychiatry* 32 (November, 1975), pp. 1394–1398.

Sobczynski, Anna. "The 'Big 2' Strengthen Their Grip." *Advertis-*

ing Age, March 29, 1982, pp. M37–M41.

Speiglman, Richard, and Weisner, Connie. "Accommodation to Coercion: Changes in Alcoholism Treatment Paradigms." Paper presented at the Annual Meeting for the Study of Social Problems, San Francisco, July, 1982.

Spiegelhalder, B., et al. "Volatile Nitrosamines in Food." *Oncology* 37 (1980): 211–216.

Spieker, Gisela. "Educating Prisoners About Problems Related to Alcohol/Drug Abuse." In *Papers of the 28th International Institute on the Prevention and Treatment of Alcoholism*. Lausanne: International Council on Alcohol and Addictions, 1982.

Sullivan, Ann, et al. "Variables Related to Outcome of Treatment for Inpatient Alcoholics." *Alcohol Health and Research World*, Fall, 1981, pp. 58–60.

Swenson, Paul. "Results of a Longitudinal Evaluation of Court-Mandated DWI Treatment Programs in Phoenix, Arizona." *Journal of Studies on Alcohol* 42, no. 7 (1981), pp. 642–654.

Tabakoff, Boris. "Research Advances in Understanding the Biology of Alcohol Intoxication and Tolerance." In *Papers of the 28th International Institute on the Prevention and Treatment of Alcoholism*. Lausanne: International Council on Alcohol and Addictions, 1982.

"Trial Judges' Conference, Sponsored by Creative Alternatives to Prison." In *Committee on the Judiciary, U.S. Senate*. Washington, D.C.: U.S. Government Printing Office, October 14, 1978, pp. 8–9.

Turner, Thomas, M.D. "Real Alcoholics Don't Drink Beer." *Modern Brewery Age*, April-May, 1982, pp. MS74–MS97.

Tuyns, Albert. "Alcohol and Cancer." *Alcohol Health and Research World*, Summer, 1978, pp. 20–31.

Valverius, Milan. "Alcohol and Criminality." In *Papers of the 28th International Institute on the Prevention and Treatment of Alcoholism*. Lausanne: International Council on Alcohol and Addictions, 1982.

Waahlberg, Ragnar. "November 14, 1981 — Report on a Mass Media Attempt to Change Behavior." Unpublished paper, the Norwegian Directorate of Alcohol and Drug Problems, n.d.

Wechsler, H. "Extensive Users of Alcohol Among College Students." *Journal of Studies on Alcohol* 42 (1981), pp. 150–155.

Westermeyer, Joseph, et al. "An Evaluation of Alcoholism Services in Minnesota Using a Social Indicator Method." *American Journal of Public Health* 70, no. 11 (November, 1980), pp. 1209–1211.

Woodside, Migs. "Children of Alcoholics: A Report to Gov. Hugh L. Carey." New York State Division of Alcoholism and Alcohol Abuse, July, 1982.

Worden, Mark. "In Defense of Neoprohibitionism." *Alcoholism,* May-June, 1982, p. 51.

INDEX

Abrahams, Dr. Andrew, 97

Abram, Morris B., 141

Abscam trials, 111-12, 158

Addiction Research Foundation, 10, 43

Adelman, Martin, 90-92

Adlai, Richard, 35, 40

Advertising, *see* Media; Moderate, healthy drinking; New public policies

Advertising Age, 41

Alcohol abuse
  awareness of, 1, 4-5, 73, 77, 148-50
  costs, 2, 63, 66, 69, 76
  defined, 1
  drinking for euphoria v. taste, 8, 23-24, 30, 35
  history, 3
  incidence, 1-2, 73-74, 76, 115
  statistics and tragedies, 1-2, 13-14, 16-17, 62-63, 73-74, 145-47, 154
  See also Amethystic; Dealcoholized beverages; Media; Moderate, healthy drinking; National education campaign for moderate drinking; New public policies; Taxes to moderate consumption

Alcohol beverage industry
  on general health warning label, 57
  on higher beverage taxes, 50, 54
  on ingredient and calorie label, 85
  on label warning pregnant women, 238-42, 246-47
  on national education campaign, 10, 17
  Neo-prohibition charge, 11, 20, 41, 58, 60, 152
  political influence, 54-56
  power, 57
  theme: "When you're having more than one," 16
  See also Fetal alcohol syndrome; Media; New public policies, Political action

Alcohol — effects on body
  brain, 109-110
  calories, 22, 35, 145
  general, 8, 82, 86-87
  health problems, 37-38, 43, 47, 66, 145, 152-54, 157-58, 165
  public ignorance of, 16, 153, 158, 164
  See also Fetal alcohol syndrome

Alcohol and Health, 14

Alcoholic Beverage Newsletter, 23

"Alcoholic" children — test to identify
  cell membrane theory, 5, 109-10, 112
  chemical manipulation of body, 110-11
  dangers of, 112-13
  effect on criminals, 111-12
  effect on society in general, 112-13
  See also Cholesterol; Ethics; Political action

Alcoholics Anonymous (AA), 72-73, 77, 81-83, 87, 107, 112, 124, 128, 147

Alcoholism
  as addiction or illness, 4, 68-69, 74-77
  awareness of, 2, 4-5, 148-50
  causes of, 109, 111, 146
  costs, 2, 63, 69, 73-74, 76, 84-85, 113, 143
  defined, 2, 68-69

dual addiction, 112-13
incidence, 2, 8, 13, 69, 105
    113, 143, 154
nonlegal confrontation, 105-108,
    129
nutrition, 166
signs of, 82, 116, 145-47
tolerance, 68, 110
treatment in general, 118, 124,
    128, 146-47
See also "Alcoholic" children;
    Amethystic; Dealcoholized
    beverages; Drunk driving;
    National education cam-
    paign for moderate drink-
    ing; Political action, on
    warning labels
Alcoholism, 11, 36, 57, 117
Alcohol Research Group, 70, 117,
    139
Alina Lodge, 124
Allen, Dr. Gail, 45
Altman, Jack, 95
American Cancer Society's
    Smokeout, 163
American Civil Liberties Union,
    92
American Medical Association,
    164
Amethystic (sober-up pill)
    chemicals to use, 63
    effect on alcohol abusers, 3-4,
        .62-66
    effect on alcoholics, 66-67
    effect on body, 63
    effect on crime, 66
    effect on society, 3, 62, 64-67
    history of, 62
    public acceptance of, 64, 66
    spurred by drunk driver laws,
        64
    spurred by lawsuits, 64-66
ANSVAR, 58
Antabuse (disulfiram)

court-ordered use of, 70, 82-83,
    86-87, 92, 98, 102
implants of, 86-87
See also Compulsory treatment;
    Ethics
Arab nations, 101
Askew, Reubin, 142
Atkins, Dr. Robert, 32-33
Auret, Dr. A. J., 79, 103
Australia, 26, 38, 132
Austria, 89

Bähler, Dr. Veronique, 118, 138
Baker, Howard, 2
Barbera, Dr. Luigi, 32
Barrios, Peter, 124
Beaubron, Dr. Michael, 43
Beauchamp, Dan (Beyond Alco-
    holism: Alcohol and Public
    Health Policy), 11, 32, 167
Belgium, 103
Bellamy, Carol, 160, 168
Bentham, Jeremy, 122
Blane, Dr. Howard, 53
Blume, Dr. Sheila, 111-12, 131
Boston University Medical Center,
    181
Bottom Line, 25
Brandt, Dr. Edward, 164
Britain, 15, 46
Brown v. Board of Education, 15,
    46
Bruce, Paddy, 92-93
Buck v. Bell, 122

Cameron, Tracy, 150
Canada
    alcohol abuse in, 73, 113
    compulsory treatment, 85-86,
        92-95
    high alcohol taxes, 43, 48, 50
    public awareness, 165
    TV advertising, 56
Canadian Civil Liberties Associa-
    tion, 86

Cancro, Dr. Robert, 39
Carey, Hugh, 125
Carter, Jimmy, 2, 58, 152, 155-56
Catanzaro, Dr. Ronald, 71
CBS Publications, 53
Center for Science in the Public Interest, 44, 51, 60
Centers for Disease Control, 166
Chafetz, Dr. Morris, 45, 165
Cholesterol (possible relation to alcohol addiction), 111-12
Cisin, Ira, 64
Cloud, Dr. Luther, 29
Cohen, Morris R., 130
Commission for the Study of Ethical Problems in Medicine and Biomedical and Behavioral Research, 141
Committee on Nutrition of the Mother and Preschool Child, 153
Compulsory treatment
    abroad, 72-74, 88, 92-93, 103
    Antabuse, use of, 70, 82-83, 86-87, 92, 98, 102
    case examples, 82-83, 115-16, 119-20, 122-23
    compared to forced treatment, 76
    costs v. benefits, 78, 84-85, 89-90, 134
    in criminal court, 87, 96, 98-99, 101-03, 105
    with drunk drivers, 5, 69-72, 76, 78-79, 81-83, 88, 93, 97, 100, 103, 115-117
    effect on other social-health problems, 98-100
    examples of laws, 69-72, 85-87, 89, 91, 93, 96-98, 105, 173-80
    in family disputes, 71, 78-79, 85-86, 88-91, 105-08

heroin treatment, in contrast to, 93-95, 101-02
    history of, 74-77
    legal arguments over, 86, 90-92, 98-99, 102
    need to restrain, 88, 90-96, 103-04
    nonlegal confrontation, compared to, 105-08, 123-24
    and nutrition, 166
    society's motivation for, 69, 76-77, 84-85, 118
    success of, 4-5, 77-80, 82-85, 88, 91-93, 95-98, 100, 102-03, 132
    treatment offered, 78-80, 84-85, 88, 95-98
    treatment skills needed, 80-82, 84-85, 93
    with welfare recipients, 5, 69, 80, 82-83
    See also Ethics
Consumers Union, 47
Cook, Philip, 45, 47
Crime, 64, 66, 70, 73-77, 96, 98-99, 101-03, 105, 111-12, 149, 167
    See also Compulsory treatment; Ethics
Cuomo, Mario, 160
Czechoslovakia, 72, 77, 82, 85, 128-29, 135

Da Costa, J. Pinto, 74
Dachau, 136-37
Daily News (New York), 149
Davis, Rex, 165
Dealcoholized beverages
    abroad, 31-34
    alcoholism, impact on, 30, 33-35
    Alive Polarity, 41
    brands, addresses of, 41
    calories, 22, 35

Carl Jung, 41
Castella, 26, 41
Château, 41
compared to alcoholic drinks, 22
compared to decaffeinated coffee, 24, 37-38, 40, 146
compared to light beer and wine, 24-25, 30-31, 39-40
consumer tests, 5, 23, 25-30, 33, 41
contents label, 35-37
dealcoholized liquor, 30
effect on national drinking campaign, 23, 32-35, 146
Giovane, 26, 35, 40-41
Kingsbury, 26, 41
legislation needed for, 38-39
Metbrau, 26, 37, 41
as part of new drinking style, 25, 30-31, 40-41
possible negative effects on alcoholics, 33-35
production and other problems, 37-41
purchasers of, 65-74
teaching to drink for taste, 23, 30, 35
used to moderate consumption, 24
DeLuca, John A., 36
DeLuca, John R., 56, 58, 152-56
Denham-Hainsy, Maureen, 124
Denmark, 109
Department of Health and Human Services (HHS), 152-55
di Gennaro, Giuseppe, 139
Distilled Spirits Council of the United States (DISCUS), 10, 30, 42
Meister, Frederick, 50, 56
Domestic Policy Staff, 155-56
Dram Shop Act, 65-66
Drew, L. R. H., 132

Drinking
  abstainers, 25, 27, 53
  alcohol contents, 36-37
  costs of, 42-43, 46
  heavy drinkers, 14, 27-28, 31, 43, 50, 53
  moderate drinkers, 27-28, 31, 53
Drinking age (legal), 8-9, 20, 139-40
Drunk driving
  alcoholics and, 23
  amethystic's effect on, 62, 64
  laws on, 9, 20, 40
  national awareness week, 1
  national commission on, 9, 139
  nonalcohol related answers for, 166
  public's perception of, 149
  related to alcohol's costs, 42-43, 47, 49
  youth and, 2, 8-9
  See also Compulsory treatment; Ethics
Drunkenness
  cause of, 4-5
  in public, 73-77
  See also Amethystic

E. & J. Gallo Winery, 40
Eagleton, Thomas, 44
Eagleville Hospital, 101-02
East Germany, 102, 136-38
Easter, DeWitt, 75
Egypt, 73
Eizenstat, Stuart, 156
Employee alcoholism programs, 4, 76-77, 106, 123, 128-29, 150
Emrick, Dr. Chad, 87
England, 75, 151
Englemann, Larry (Intemperance), 18, 49
Epstein, Thomas, 102
Erasmus, 21

Ethics
  adjournment of compulsory treat-
    ment, 131
  autonomy, protection of, 120-
    22
  compulsory Antabuse, 124,
    127-28, 135
  compulsory treatment and court
    appeal, 130-31
  compulsory treatment and crimi-
    nals, 127-28, 133
  compulsory treatment and drunk
    drivers, 5, 115-16, 122-23,
    128, 130, 133
  compulsory treatment and family
    disputes, 118, 121, 123,
    125-28, 133
  compulsory treatment and ther-
    apy offered, 132-34, 138-
    39
  compulsory treatment and wel-
    fare poor, 5, 119-21, 123-
    25, 128-33
  compulsory treatment for person
    harming only himself, 128-
    29, 135-36
  individual rights theory, 119-21,
    123-24, 127, 135
  model compulsory treatment
    law, 130-36
  national education campaign,
    114
  need for, 114-15
  new public policies (consump-
    tion limits, drinking age,
    taxes), 114, 139-40
  opinions in international survey,
    124-25, 127-30, 176-78
  test to identify "alcoholic"
    children, 114, 140-41
  utilitarian theory, 122-23, 125,
    127, 129, 132, 135-39
Evans, David, 126

Faden, Ruth, 140
Families
  effects of alcohol on, 2, 68-69
  help from coercive treatment,
    71, 78-79, 85-86, 88-91,
    105-08, 117-18
  politically involved, 160-61
  public's perceptions of, 148-50
  See also Compulsory treatment;
    Ethics
Farber, Leslie, 47
Fetal alcohol syndrome
  incidence, 119, 153, 164-65
  laws to prevent, 153-56, 158,
    164-66
Field Research Corporation poll,
    149-50
Finland
  compulsory treatment, 72, 125
  dealcoholized beverages, 32
  taxes and other controls, 43, 48-
    49, 59
Food and Drug Administration
    (FDA), 24, 67, 156
Ford, Betty, 2, 108
Ford, Gerald, 2, 62
France, 15, 41, 151, 159
Friedman, Francis X., 142

Gacic, Branko, 128
Gallanter, Marc, 16
Galbraith, John Kenneth, 167
Gallup, George, Jr., 149
Gallup survey
  alcohol beverage industry's
    reaction to, 156
  Bezilla, Robert, 157
  comparing drinking to smoking,
    diet and exercise, 9-10, 22,
    148
  effect of taxes on consumption,
    59
  Gallup Youth Survey, 148-49
  support of higher alcohol taxes,

50, 161
support of politicians and parties,
148, 160
See also Appendix B
Gateway Community Services, 81
Geller, Dr. Anne, 67, 110-11
G. Heileman Brewing Company,
23
Goldstein, Dr. Dora, 110-11
Goodstadt, Michael, 50
Goodwin, Donald, 109
Gordis, Dr. Enoch, 78
Greizerstein, Hebe, 36
Grider, Barbara, 98
Gunn, Dr. John, 101

Hammond, Robert, 53
Hanrahan, Michael, 81
Harris (Louis) poll, 149
Harris, Patricia, 155
Hathaway, William, 56
Hazelden Treatment Center, 78-
79, 134
Health awareness and drinking, 3,
17, 21-22, 25, 35, 40-41,
143-46
Health Promotion Foundation, 28
Hinderer, Dr. Hans, 102
Hingson, Ralph, 118
Hinkle, Richard Paul, 30, 41
Hoffman, Norman, 89
Holden, William, 16
Holland, 72
Home breathalyzers, 66
Homeless — changing attitude
toward, 99
Hughes, Harold, 159
Humphrey, Gordon, 164-65
Hungary, 57, 131

India, 58
Inherently dangerous product
theory, 157-58
International Council on Alcohol

and Addictions, 72, 77, 124
Iraq, 73
Israel, 8, 60-61
Israel, Dr. Yedy, 87, 110
Italians, 8, 14-15, 17
Italy, 25, 34, 74

Jacobs, Michael, 79
Jacobson, Michael, 51, 60
Javits, Jacob, 152
Jews, 8, 14-15, 17, 19
Johnson, Nicholas, 56
The Journal (Toronto), 94

Kant, Immanuel, 121, 135
Kean, Tom, 71, 126
Kelly, Patricia, 165
Kennedy, Ted, 2
Kittrie, Nicholas, 98
Koch, Ed, 160
Kramer, Hilton, 54
Krimmel, Herman, 104
Kübler-Ross, Elisabeth, 16

Lakeville Journal (Conn.), 132
Leake, Jim, 95-96
Lipsig, Harry, 65
Lowenstein, Ralph, 9

McClelland, Robert, 94
Maimonides, 19
Maine — tax hike, 54-55
Manning, Thomas, 25
Marco, Dr. Corey, 92
Marx, Karl, 56, 140
Matzner, Joseph (*Beverage Re-
tailer*), 156
Max Planck Institute, 129
May, Ernest, 168
Mayer, William, 1
Media
coverage of alcohol abuse and
alcoholism, 7-9, 51-54
drinking styles portrayed, 14-15

effect of alcohol industry adver-
    tising, 15, 52-54, 155
Mendès-France, Pierre, 159
Menninger, Dr. Karl, 98
Mill, John Stuart, 122
Miller, Jerauld, 117
Mills, Wilbur, 2, 54-55
Moderate, healthy drinking
    definition of, 14
    limits of, 8, 15
    media's effect on, 14-15
    and new health awareness, 4,
        17, 21-23, 25, 35, 40-41,
        60
    personal habits to achieve, 15,
        52
    present public drinking habits, 8-
        9, 14, 52
    rules for, 143-47
    and women, 7
    See also Alcohol — effects on
        body; Dealcoholized bev-
        erages; National education
        campaign for moderate
        drinking; Political action
Moral Majority, 3, 60
Morawski, Jacek, 88, 150
Morehouse, Ellen, 80-81
Morris, Herbert, 136
Mosher, James, 151
Moskalewicz, Jacek, 151
Myers Act, 133

National education campaign for
    moderate drinking
    bases for, 14-15
    effect on alcohol abuse, 3, 13
    effect on alcoholics, 3, 13, 19
    goals of, 14, 18-19, 42
    new drinking suggestions and
        values, 15-18
    new learned instinct, 17
    opposition to, 10-11, 17-19

role of culturally accepted limits,
    7, 17-18
uncertainty of politicans toward,
    21
See also Ethics
National Highway Traffic Adminis-
    tration, 100
National Institute on Alcohol
    Abuse and Alcoholism
    (NIAAA), 2, 13-14, 58, 66,
    69, 101, 147, 152, 159
National Research Council
    (Alcohol and Public Policy:
    Beyond the Shadow of Pro-
    hibition), 5, 43-45, 47, 104
National Unification Church, 16
Nazi era, 94, 129, 136-38
New Health, 60
New public policies
    advertising restrictions, 56-57,
        59
    cost of alcoholic beverages, 42-
        43
    drinking age, 8-9, 20
    higher taxes, 42-51
    joining other social-health issues,
        59-61
    opposition to, 44-46, 48, 54-
        56
    start of, 50-56, 59
    warning labels and signs, 11, 35-
        37, 57-58
    See also Ethics; Gallup
        survey; Taxes
Newsweek, 52
New York Civil Liberties Union,
    99
New Yorker, The, 89
New York State Human Rights
    Commission, 136
New York Times, 100
New Zealand, 103
Noble, Dr. Ernest, 56, 62-64, 67
North, Stephen, 74

Norway
  in general, 32, 40-41, 48, 72-73, 87
  give-up-alcohol-for-one-night campaign, 161-63
Nutrition and drinking, 262-63

Occupational Health and Safety, 158
Ogilvy & Mather, 52-53
Oktoberfest, 32
Orientals, 14
Orwell, George (*1984*), 48

Paley, Marlene, 79-80, 100
"Patriot's Prayer, The" (Lippman), 18
Peltoniemi, Teuvo, 125
Perrin, Thomas, 121
Petropoulos, Alice, 82, 119
Phillips, Dr. Michael, 86
Pioneer Center North, 95-96, 132
Pittman, David, 10, 17
Plato, 114
Poland
  compulsory treatment, 72, 88
  more taxes and controls, 43
  See also Solidarity
Political action
  alcohol beverage industry opposition to, 151-56, 164-65, 167
  on alcohol availability generally, 150
  combined with other social-health issues, 10, 59-61, 158, 167-68
  discomfort of politicians, 20-21, 51, 54, 142-43
  give-up alcohol day, 161-63
  on higher taxes, 150, 161
  influence of individual drinking behaviors, 143-47
  lobbying power of alcohol

industry, 154-56
  a moderate drinking campaign, 23, 50, 156, 161-63
  proof of public support for, 148-50, 159-60, 169
  sparked by test to identify "alcoholic" children, 161
  the catalyst issue, 157-66
  through lawsuits, 157-58
  on warning labels and posters, 57-58, 152-58, 164-66
  See also Alcohol beverage industry; Moderate, healthy drinking, rules for; Solidarity
Portugal, 73
Press-Telegram (Long Beach, Cal.), 25
Progressivism, 168
Prohibition
  fatalism of, 13
  health effects of, 49
  negative effects of, 17, 18, 44
  rigid values of, 12, 19
  as symbol of change, 60, 168
Prohibition Party, 59

Raspberry, William, 48
Reactive drinking, 146-47
Reagan, Ronald, 1-2, 9, 43-44, 48, 152, 156
"Red head," defined, 36
Rexed, Bror, 73
Richards, David A., 120
Richmond, Dr. Julius, 154
Rinella, Vincent, 101-02
Room, Robin, 103, 117, 139-40
Roselius, Dr. Ludwig, 39
Rosellini, Gayle, 81, 128

Sanka, 40
Sapontzis, S. F., 119
Schukit, Marc, 86
Schulte, Bernd, 129

Schuster, Erich, 31
Screvane, Paul, 20
Shanken, Marvin, 25
Shannon, John, 102
Shaughnessy, John, 94
Siegel, Ronald, 113
Simpson, Dr. Lance, 101
Skála, Dr. Jaroslav, 77, 82, 93
Smithers, Brinkley, 144
Smithers, Francis, 28
Sober-Aid, 67
Solidarity, 150-51
Somali, 73
South Africa, 79, 88-89, 103, 138-39
Soviet Union, 56
Spieker, Gisela, 127
Stevenson, Leon, 168-69
Striani, Dr. Daniele, 74
Sweden, 58, 73, 87, 100
Swenson, Paul, 93
Switzerland, 33
Szent-Györgi, Albert, 62

Tabakoff, Dr. Boris, 111
Taxes to moderate consumption
    effect on alcohol abusers, 3, 42-50
    effect on alcoholics, 45, 50
    effect on drunk driving, 43, 47
    effect on health problems, 47-49
    effect on poor, 47-48, 51
    effect on present drinking levels, 45-46, 53
    effect on taxpayers, 50, 56
    increase desired, 44, 46, 52
    media reaction to, 52-54
    opposition to, 44-46, 48, 50, 54-56
    present tax levels, 44
    relation to alcohol's cost, 42-43, 46
    sensitivity of issue, 51, 54-55

support for, 44-45, 47-48, 50
    See also Ethics; New public policies; Political action
Terris, Milton, 11
Texas Select, 23, 29
Thomey, Tedd, 25
Thurmond, Strom, 152
Time, 52
Totino, Bob, 95
"Tough love," defined, 81
Treasury Department
    health hazards report, 16, 38, 145
    ingredient label, 37
    warning labels, 57, 152-55
Triantafillou, Dr. Mark, 85-86
Trinidad, 43
Tucker, John, 159

United Arab Emirates, 73
U.S. Brewers Association, 26, 39, 58
U.S. Journal, 46, 52
U.S. News & World Report, 52

Valley Express, The (Iowa), 12-13
Valverius, Milan, 101
Vietnam vets, 118
Villa Banfi, 30
Volpe, John, 9

Waahlberg, Ragnar, 162
Wagner, Robert, Jr., 142-43
Walthew, Janet Page, 96
Washington Post, 48, 75
Wegscheider, Sharon, 123-24
Welfare, see Compulsory treatment; Ethics
West Germany, 31-32, 37, 41, 78, 88, 103, 129, 136-38
Westermeyer, Dr. Joseph, 13
Williams, Harrison, 158
Wilson, Edmund (To the Finland

Station), 140
Wine Institute, 26, 36
Women, 7, 146-47
   See also Fetal alcohol syndrome
Wood, Natalie, 16
Worden, Mark, 11
World   Health   Organization
      (WHO)
   on alcohol abuse in developing
      nations, 73
   on changing role of government,
      10, 49
   on higher taxes, 44
   on new drinking values, 15-16
   on treatment for alcoholics, 134,
      139

Youth
   compulsory treatment of, 79,
      98, 100, 129
   drinking styles of, 23, 31, 35,
      44
   and drunken accidents, 2, 8
   influence of parents, 8, 35
Yugoslavia, 128

Ziegler, Dr. Herbert, 78, 88

Acknowledgments

The author is grateful for the personal support from: Karen, Rachel and David. My parents and Thelma. David Kriser, Dr. Nicholas Pace, Brinkley Smithers, Francis Smithers, and the board of directors and staff of The New York City Affiliate of the National Council on Alcoholism. The members of the Legal Issues Section of the International Council on Alcohol and Addictions. The Health Promotion Foundation. Marie Cantlon. And especially Gerry Goodman.

Allan Luks is executive director of The New York City Affiliate of the National Council on Alcoholism and adjunct professor at Fordham University Graduate School of Social Services.

Well known as a writer and lecturer on alcohol abuse, Luks is also Chairman of the Legal Issues Section of the International Council on Alcohol and Addictions, and serves on the Alliance on Crime Prevention and Criminal Justice, which has nongovernmental organization status at the United Nations.

In addition to numerous articles on public issues for newspapers and magazines, Luks has edited *Having Been There,* a book of short stories on alcoholism's human drama.